MEETINGS

Rules

&

Procedures

Alice N. Pohl

NTC Business Books
a division of *NTC Publishing Group* • Lincolnwood, Illinois USA

About the Author

From her many years of experience as teacher and consultant, Alice N. Pohl has acquired a practical insight into the questions and problems confronting all types of organizations regarding parliamentary procedure.

Pohl is the Accrediting Director for the American Institute of Parliamentarians. She is the author of several books and a variety of articles on parliamentary procedure.

9 0 ML 9 8 7 6 5 4 3 2 1

Preface

Meetings are one of the most complex activities you "do." The success or failure of a meeting has a significant impact on you and your group. When things go wrong in a meeting, does your group stop and analyze what has happened? Do you know and practice the fundamentals of a meeting? Even though you may attend many meetings, you may not have had any formal training in how to conduct or participate in them.

This book is a new approach to meetings. It provides a clear, logical text for organizations. The material is arranged so that readers can easily progress from one subject to another.

In these days, when society is organized as never before, the best results can only be accomplished by means of the skill of working together. Parliamentary procedure is a tool that enables an assembly to discuss a problem with full and free debate and to take definite action. Parliamentary law provides a means of transacting an organization's business accurately, justly, and expeditiously.

There is probably no subject more universally misunderstood than parliamentary law. I have received countless requests from organizations seeking my assistance in resolving some parliamentary problem. I have always tried to be helpful. I can now refer persons making inquiry to this book, *Meetings: Rules & Procedures,* for in it I have attempted to provide simplified parliamentary procedure that can be understood by anyone, whether president or member. The careful reading and use of this material can guarantee orderliness and fair play in a meeting.

–A. N. P.

Contents

Part One

Formal Meetings
How to Preside and Participate

Chapter 1

Meetings and Sessions

A *meeting* is a single gathering of an organization's members in one area to transact business. A *session* is a meeting or series of meetings devoted to a single order of business, a program, an agenda, or any other announced purpose; when there is more than one meeting, each succeeding meeting continues the business at the point where it was left off. This part of *Meetings: Rules & Procedures* is designed to help readers use parliamentary procedure to most effectively participate in meetings and sessions, both as officers and as members of an organization.

The Basics of Parliamentary Procedure

Every decision-making body has some rules that it has adopted. These rules apply whenever the group makes a decision. If the group fails to conform to them, the decision becomes invalid. Similarly, every member of a group is presumed to be equal and to have rights that must be protected. If members do not make appropriate use of their rights, however, they may lose them.

Parliamentary procedure is a set of formalized rules for decision-making groups. The rules have been developed to expedite business and to help organizations carry out their aims. Parliamentary procedure makes it easier for the members of an organization to work together harmoniously and to protect the rights of the majority, the minority, and the absentee.

The principles of parliamentary procedure are simple and logical. They include the following:

1. The organization must meet to make a decision. Proper notice of the meeting, including the time, place, and purpose, must be given to all members of the organization.

2. There must be a quorum present at the meeting.

3. The decision that the organization makes must be based on some question. The question may be written or spoken. Members have the right to know what the question is and what its effects will be before they vote on it.

4. There must be opportunity to debate the question. It is a member's right to hear and to be heard.

5. The question must be decided by taking a vote. With a few exceptions, the majority position in the vote becomes the decision of the organization. No member can be compelled to vote; however, anyone who does not vote has the effect of voting with the prevailing side.

6. Any decision reached is considered null and void if it is in conflict with any higher authority, such as the

constitution, bylaws, or other rules of the organization, or any national, state, or local law.

7. The decision belongs to the majority, but the rights to discuss, to be heard, and to oppose are valued rights of the minority. These rights must be protected.

8. If a subject has been voted on, it may not be presented again in the same form. The only way to bring a subject back for consideration at the same meeting is to move to reconsider the vote taken on the subject.

These eight rules are the most basic components of parliamentary procedure. Everything else builds on these components to ensure that the goals and rights of a group are met. This section of *Meetings: Rules & Procedures* is dedicated to showing you how parliamentary procedure fits together, so that you can use it confidently and effectively in formal meeting situations, whether you are the presiding officer, the secretary, or one of the other members.

Conducting a Meeting

The officers required to conduct a meeting are the presiding officer and the secretary. The minimum number of persons who must be present at a meeting for a business to be legally transacted is the quorum of the membership. The quorum refers to the number present, and not to the number actually voting on a particular question.

Meetings may include three parts: the opening, which may include a prayer (if appropriate), pledge to the flag, song, welcome, or introductions; the business; and the closing, which may include a program or speaker. The business portion of the meeting includes the agenda—all the subjects that must be attended to, and the order in which they are to be considered.

Order of Business

The essential parts of a business meeting are (1) call to order; (2) minutes; (3) reports of officers, boards, and committees; (4) unfinished business; (5) new business; and (6) adjournment. Table 1.1 shows a typical order of business. The regular order of business should be followed, allowing for reasonable flexibility. There is no standard rule for including other topics in the order of business. Each organization decides where it inserts these items.

Table 1.1

Typical Order of Business

Reading and approval of minutes
Reports of officers
Reports of boards (cabinet, council, executive committee)
Reports of standing committees
Reports of special committees
Special orders (orders that were not disposed of at the previous meeting)
Unfinished business
New business

Some organizations include "good of the order" or "organization welfare" after new business. This allows for specific suggestions, constructive comments, criticism, or compliments. No motions may be proposed during this time.

The order of business for a special meeting consists only of the call to order, consideration of the items stated in the notice of the meeting, and adjournment.

Sample Agenda

The agenda of a meeting governs the business that must be attended to during that meeting. The items included in a typical agenda are covered below. Any item of business on the agenda can be taken out of order by adopting a motion to suspend the rules. This motion requires a two-thirds vote or general consent.

Call to Order.   The presiding officer calls the meeting to order promptly at the scheduled time with one tap of the gavel. The secretary then ascertains whether or not a quorum is present. If a quorum is not present, business cannot be legally conducted at the meeting.

Reading and Approval of Minutes.   The first business in order is reading and approving the minutes of the previous meeting. After corrections have been made, the minutes are approved as corrected. Corrections may be approved by general consent. If the organization has a committee to correct and approve the minutes, the chair announces the fact.

Reports of Officers.   At an annual meeting, the officers report in the order in which they are listed in the bylaws of the organization. At regular meetings, the presiding officer usually calls on the treasurer to report first. The treasurer reports the income and expenses since the previous meeting. The presiding officer then asks if there are any questions. After the treasurer answers the questions, the presiding officer states that the report will be placed on file. No vote is taken on the treasurer's report.

Reports of Committees.   The report of the board of directors or governing body is given first. A summary of the action taken by the board may be given. If the board presents a recommendation, it is considered and voted upon at this time. No second from the assembly is required.

Only those standing committees with a report to give should be called upon. Written reports are worded in the third person ("the committee determined"). No action is taken on an informational report.

If there is a nominating committee, it makes its report after the other standing committees. No vote is taken on the nominating committee's report.

Special committees that are to report are called on in the order in which they were appointed.

Special Orders.   Items of business that have been made special orders are taken in the order in which they were made. A *special order* is an item of business that must be considered at a certain time because the assembly has voted to consider it then.

General Orders and Unfinished Business.   A *general order* is any question that, usually by postponement, has been made an order of the day without being made a special order. *Unfinished business* is a question that was pending when the previous meeting adjourned, a question that was unfinished at the previous meeting, or a matter that was postponed. The chair should not ask for unfinished business. He or she should have a list of all subjects.

An item that was laid on the table (in order to attend to more pressing business) may be taken from the table at this time or under new business.

New Business. Correspondence which requires action should be brought up at this time. Items laid on the table also may be brought up, since they are not automatically on the agenda. Additionally, members may introduce new items of business.

Announcements. The chair may make, or call upon another member to make, any necessary announcements. After the announcements, the chair may adjourn the meeting. No motion is necessary.

Quorum

Since it is seldom possible to have every member present at each meeting, it is necessary to allow a certain proportion of the membership, the *quorum*, to transact the business of the organization. If a majority of the membership is present, business can be transacted, regardless of the number of members actually voting.

The number that constitutes a quorum is usually stated in the constitution or bylaws of the organization. The quorum should be based on the number of members that can be depended on to be present at any meeting. If there is no provision for what constitutes a quorum, the quorum is a majority of the total membership of the organization. The requirement of a quorum is a protection against unrepresentative action by a small number of persons. It is a legal and common practice to fix the quorum at less than a majority of the membership. If the provision for a quorum is a small proportion of the total membership, rigid requirements for notices of meetings should be established, so that all members will have an opportunity to be present.

When there is no provision for a quorum in the bylaws, common parliamentary law determines the quorum as follows:

1. In a mass meeting, the quorum is those present.

2. In ordinary organizations whose bylaws do not specify a quorum, the quorum is a majority of all members.

3. In a conference or convention in which there are delegates, unless provided otherwise, the quorum is a majority of qualified delegates who have been registered as attending, whether or not some have left.

4. In organizations in which there are no required dues, and for which the membership list may not be reliable, the quorum of those attending the meeting.

5. In committees or boards, the quorum is a majority of the members of the committee or board. A committee or board does not have the power to determine its quorum, unless the bylaws authorize it.

Proceedings in the Absence of a Quorum

If the organization's rules require that a meeting be held, the absence of a quorum does not prevent calling the meeting to order. The minutes must show that the rules were complied with and the meeting held.

The only actions that can be legally transacted in the absence of a quorum are the following:

- To fix the time of adjournment

- To adjourn

- To take a recess in order to try to obtain a quorum

Regular business cannot be transacted in the absence of a quorum. However, emergency action can be taken and confirmed or approved at the next meeting. The motion to *ratify* (approve or confirm) is used to validate an action already taken without a quorum present.

While business cannot legally be transacted in the absence of a quorum, a quorum is not required for certain actions. Committee reports can be received for information (but no action may be taken on them). The program of the day also can be given.

When a member notices the absence of a quorum, he or she can make a point of order to that effect at any time, as long as the point of order does not interrupt the person speaking. When the chair notices the absence of a quorum, he or she can entertain a motion to adjourn or to take a recess to contact members and ask them to attend. In organizations that have the power to compel members to attend, a "call of the house" can be ordered.

The quorum for all meetings should be established in a section of the bylaws. An amendment to the bylaws goes into effect immediately upon its adoption. The proper procedure to amend that part of the bylaws is to strike out the old provision or number and insert the new provision. This should be made and voted upon as one motion. If the number is simply struck, the quorum instantly becomes a majority of the membership.

Motions

A *motion* is a formal statement of a proposal for consideration by the assembly. The essential steps by which a motion is brought before the assembly are listed below:

1. A member rises, addresses the chair, then waits for recognition.

2. The chair recognizes the member.

3. The member proposes the motion by saying, "I move that . . . ."

4. Another member seconds the motion without rising or addressing the chair. A second implies the seconder wishes the motion to be considered by the assembly. It does not indicate that the seconder favors the motion; he or she may wish to speak against it or vote against it. If a motion is not seconded, it is not considered before the assembly. The chair proceeds to the next item of business.

5. The chair states the motion, which then becomes the question: "It is moved and seconded that . . . . Is there any discussion?" If the wording is not clear, the chair should put it into suitable form. The motion should be recorded in the minutes as the chair has stated it.

6. During discussion, speakers must: be entitled to the floor; address their remarks to the chair, be courteous, and avoid speaking about personalities; confine the discussion to the pending question; observe the rules as to the number of times and length of time a speaker may speak to a question; ask for information; this is not counted as debate.

7. The chair puts the question by saying, "Those in favor of the motion that . . . say Aye. Those opposed,

say No." The chair always must call for the negative vote and tell the assembly what to say. If the voice vote is in doubt, a rising vote or show of hands may be taken.

8. The chair must announce the result of the vote. If the vote is tied, the motion is lost. The chair may vote to make or break a tie vote.

Assumed Motions

Because the presiding officer is responsible for expediting business, the chair may *assume the motion*, that is, state the question without waiting for a formal motion by a member.

For example, after the reading of the minutes, the chair may simply state, "The minutes are approved as read." If a committee presents a special report, the chair may say, "The question is on the adoption of the committee's recommendation. Is there any discussion?"

General Consent

In routine business or matters of little importance, where there seems to be no objection, time often can be saved by using *general consent* (also called *unanimous consent*).

To obtain general consent, the chair states, "If there is no objection" or "Is there any objection to . . . ?" The chair then pauses and continues, "Hearing no objection, we will . . . ." If anyone does call out "Objection," the chair formally states the question and takes a vote to determine the result.

General consent does not imply that every member is in favor of the proposed action; it means that the opposition may feel it is useless to oppose or discuss the matter.

For example, if a speaker's time in debate has expired and he or she asks for additional time, the chair may say, "If there is no objection, the member's time will be extended."

Amendments to motions are sometimes so simple or acceptable that they may be adopted by general consent. The chair may say, "If there is no objection, the words . . . will be inserted; the wording of the motion then will be . . . ."

Chapter 2

The Presiding Officer

The most important officer in a decision-making organization is the presiding officer. The exact title of the presiding officer is usually designated in the bylaws of the organization. That person may be designated "president," "chair," "chief," "moderator," or "executive officer."

The word *president* comes from the Latin word *praesidere*, which means "one who presides or is in charge of a meeting." By custom, the president never refers to him- or herself as "I" while presiding. Instead, the president uses the word chair—meaning the seat of office or authority—as in, "The chair recognizes Ms. West."

Presiding is an art. It is a combination of tact, understanding, and awareness. The president should be able to draw out ideas from the members of the group, to make them feel free and comfortable in participating in the discussion. However, the president also should be able to maintain control of the meeting and to keep it focused. A major cause of confusion in any meeting is a president who fails to keep members informed about pending business.

Although a president's specific role and responsibilities usually are stated in the bylaws of the organization, some responsibilities are common to all group leaders.

First, presidents must train themselves to speak up. A presiding officer should make sure that those sitting in the rear of the room are able to hear what is going on. Conversely, presiding officers must train themselves to be good listeners. Presidents should always remain neutral, listening to the voice of the minority and obeying the will of the majority.

Second, presidents must be able to exercise good judgment, common sense, and tact. They should be impartial, courteous, and fair—regardless of how other participants are behaving. Presiding officers should keep in mind that they have been elected or appointed to guide the affairs of the organization. A president is not chosen to be a passive observer—but she or he is not chosen to be a dictator, either.

Third, presidents should be well-versed in the organization's bylaws and standing rules. Presiding officers should always be prepared to answer any questions that may arise concerning the organization. They also should be prepared to retain what is good and discard what is bad about past practices. Tradition for tradition's sake is not always wise.

Finally, presiding officers must have precise knowledge of parliamentary procedure. They must be able to keep meetings moving effectively and to insure equality of opportunity in decision-making.

Duties of the President

In addition to the general responsibilities outlined above, a president has specific duties during a meeting. The duties include preparing for the meeting, calling the meeting to order, chairing the meeting, and knowing when and how to conclude it.

Preparation

One of the best ways to prepare for a major meeting is to hold a preliminary meeting. The preliminary meeting may consist of other officers and committee chairs. The purpose of the preliminary meeting is to present goals or to see that goals are set for the major meeting.

At the preliminary meeting, the *agenda* for the major meeting can be set. The agenda is the plan for the meeting, the order in which issues will be handled. The presiding officer should check with committee chairs to see if they are ready to report and to let them know the order in which they will be called upon. The presiding officer also should check with the secretary to see if there is any unfinished business from the previous meeting. The order for addressing unfinished business should be established first, then new business should be added to the agenda.

Finally, the presiding officer should assemble the materials he or she will need at the meeting. These include copies of the organization's bylaws and standing rules and a list of the standing committee chairs. If the presiding officer is not familiar with the precedence of motions, a chart of motions should be on hand. If there is a parliamentarian present at meetings, the president should consult with that person to make sure that the business is in order.

A president should always be ready well before a meeting. However, emergencies do happen. The most carefully planned agenda may have to be altered at the last minute to allow for more pressing business. Presiding officers must be flexible and honest, and keep the members informed.

Calling the Meeting to Order

The presiding officer should call the meeting to order at the appointed time. If a president is consistently late, the members will begin to come late, and schedules will continue to slide further and further back. The president should make sure that a quorum is present before beginning the meeting. The gavel may be used to call the meeting to order.

Chairing the Meeting

The presiding officer announces the business that should come before the assembly in the proper order. He or she should keep things moving. This includes recognizing members at the appropriate times and making sure they address the chair before they begin to speak. Members who attempt to speak before they are recognized by the chair should be called to order. The president also is responsible for making sure that speakers conclude their comments within designated time limits.

The president is responsible for making sure that all members understand the pending business. All motions that have been properly proposed (offered in the correct form and seconded) should be clearly stated—and repeated if necessary. If a motion is too long or complicated, the president should ask to have it submitted in writing. If members are confused about a motion, the president should impartially explain its effects.

The presiding officer does not participate in debate. If the presiding officer wishes to participate, he or she must relinquish the chair to a vice-president who is present, or to a ranking vice-president who has not spoken on the motion. If no vice-president is in the room, or if the vice-president declines to take the chair on the grounds of wishing to speak to the motion, the president must designate another member to take the chair. That person must be approved by the assembly.

One of the presiding officer's most difficult duties is restricting discussion to the question before the group. The president must be tactful in stopping discussion that does not relate to the matter at hand. One technique is to alternate between members speaking in favor of the motion and those speaking in opposition to it. If a member's position on the question is uncertain, the president should ask which side that person will speak on. Another technique for focusing the debate is to politely interrupt the speaker, repeat the motion, and state that the comments are not germane to the subject.

Another of the president's duties is to answer parliamentary inquiries and questions. She or he should decide questions of order and rule improper motions out of order. The president should be courteous when giving rulings on points of order or questions of procedure.

After a motion has been discussed, the presiding officer is responsible for putting it to a vote. The question is stated exactly, and then the vote is taken. The president should call for the negative vote, even if the vote seems to be all in the affirmative. The results of each vote should be announced clearly.

Adjourning the Meeting

The president can adjourn the meeting. No motion is necessary. However, the president should remind the members of the unfinished business before actually adjourning the meeting.

Procedure and the President

A certain number of parliamentary procedures affect only the presiding officer. The procedures are designed to ensure that the president will run meetings efficiently and democratically.

Parliamentary Motions Concerning the President

The president relinquishes the chair when he or she wishes to participate in the debate. There are a few exceptions to this rule. When the president is a candidate for reelection or has been nominated to be a delegate, he or she continues to preside.

However, if a motion is made requesting the resignation of the president, the chair should be relinquished to the vice-president. Similarly, if a motion is made that refers to the president in a capacity not shared with other members, he or she should relinquish the chair.

Voting Rights of the President

So that the presiding officer's vote does not unduly influence the rest of the assembly, certain parliamentary procedures govern how the president may vote.

The president does not join in a voice vote. Similarly, in a standing or show-of-hands vote, the president does not participate in the first count.

On the other hand, the president does vote when the vote is taken by ballot. The president also participates in a roll-call vote, but he or she votes last.

The president may vote when the vote will affect the results, that is, when the president's vote will cause a tie and defeat the motion or will make or break the required two-thirds. However, the president is not obliged to cast the vote that will affect the result.

Other Rights of the President

Holding office does not deprive the president of the rights of a member. However, the impartiality required of the chair precludes exercising these rights while presiding. As noted above, the president has the right to vacate the chair in order to participate in a debate. On an appeal, the president has the right to remain in the chair. In these instances, the president may speak twice—first and last.

By virtue of the office, the president is an *ex-officio* member of committees only if designated in the bylaws. This means the president has the same rights as other committee members, but he or she is not required to attend committee meetings and is not counted when determining a quorum. The ex- officio authority cannot be delegated to the vice-president or another member.

Presidential Protocol

Parliamentary procedure calls for the presiding officer to follow certain protocol. The protocol dictates when the president stands, sits, and leaves the chair.

According to protocol, the president stands for the following:

- Calling the meeting to order

- Adjourning the meeting

- Stating the question

- Putting the question to the assembly

- Explaining reasons for rulings on points of order

- Speaking on a point of order or an appeal

The president is seated or steps back from the lectern or microphone when the floor is assigned to another member.

Since no action is usually taken, the president does not leave the chair to make his or her report. The exception to this rule is when the report contains a resolution. In this case, the president would leave the chair until the resolution has been decided by the members.

Parliamentary Phrases

The presiding officer must be well versed in parliamentary procedure. To ensure the confidence of the members, the presiding officer should be careful to word motions and business properly. Some of the most useful parliamentary phrases are listed here:

- The meeting will please come to order.

- The secretary will read the minutes of the _____ meeting.

- We will now hear the _____ report.

- Are there any questions concerning the _____ report?

- The first business in order is . . . .

- The next business in order is . . . .

- New business is now in order.

- The chair recognizes . . . .

- It is moved and seconded that . . . .

- It is moved and seconded to amend the motion by . . . .

- Hearing no second, the motion is not before you at this time.

- The motion is not in order at this time.

- Please repeat your motion.

- Those in favor of the motion . . . please say Aye.

- Those opposed to the motion, say No.

- The Ayes have it; the motion is carried.

- The Ayes have it; the amendment is carried. Is there further discussion on the motion as amended?

- If there is no objection, the chair will . . . .

- For what reason does the member rise?

- If there is no further business, the meeting is adjourned.

Restrictions on Presidential Power

Parliamentary procedure contains a number of restrictions on presidential power. These restrictions exist as a check on the presiding officer.

If the presiding officer will not be able to attend a meeting, he or she cannot authorize another member to preside. The substitute must be chosen by the members. Similarly, the presiding officer cannot conduct official business by phone—except by conference phone.

During a meeting, the president has a number of restrictions on his or her actions. The presiding officer cannot do the following:

- Ask for a second to a motion

- Close debate, so long as any member who has not exhausted his or her right to speak still desires the floor

- Vote twice—once as a member and again as presiding officer

- Depart from the prescribed order of business once the agenda has been adopted by the members

- Debate while in the chair, except on an appeal

- Take from the table a motion that was laid on the table

- Take sides

- Take a voice vote if the bylaws require a ballot vote

- Declare a vote unanimous unless the motion was voted on by ballot and there are no negative votes

- Impose a penalty or order an offending member from the meeting

The President-Elect

Some organizations elect a president one term in advance. In such a case, the members do not vote for a candidate for the office of president. Instead, they elect a *president-elect* and the other officers of the organization. The president-elect automatically becomes the president in the next term. This office exists only if provided for in the bylaws.

Once a person has been elected president-elect, the organization cannot alter the decision regarding the succession or vacate the office for other reasons.

The president-elect may assume the duties of the president when that officer is absent or incapacitated; however, this must be provided for in the bylaws. If this provision has not been made, the first vice-president presides and completes the president's term.

The Past President

A *past president* is one who has served to the end of a term or has died before the expiration of that term.

If the bylaws of an organization state that the *immediate* past president automatically becomes a member of the board, only the person who served as president at the end of that term may serve.

Ex-Officio

In some organizations, the bylaws provide that the president is an ex-officio member of all committees except the nominating committee. This gives the president the same rights as the other committee members; however, he or she is not required to attend the meetings and is not counted in determining a quorum.

In some organizations, the board includes other ex-officio members. These persons are members of the board because they hold a particular office or a committee chair. An ex-officio member has the same rights, responsibilities, and duties as other members, including the right to vote.

Chapter 3

The Secretary

Although there are many kinds of secretaries, the simple term *secretary* usually means the recording secretary. In some organizations, this officer is called the clerk or recorder. This chapter is concerned only with the recording secretary.

Secretaries handle a variety of details in addition to being in charge of the records, minutes of the meeting, and related affairs of the organization. The secretary is an official who sits close to the presiding officer and observes all the proceedings carefully. By taking notes, the secretary is able to explain at any time what business is pending. As a member of the organization, the secretary does not forfeit any rights of membership. He or she retains the right to make motions, enter into discussion, and vote.

The secretary should have an understanding of the purpose of the organization and the procedures used to accomplish its goals. The secretary also must keep legible minutes, letters, and other records. The ability to read aloud effectively is another valuable skill.

Duties of the Secretary

The duties of the secretary may include preparing the agenda, presiding when necessary, taking notes, and keeping the secretary's book. Secretaries also may have other duties.

Order of Business and Agenda

Matters to be brought up at a meeting usually are known in advance. By preparing a list of topics as an outline, the secretary can help avoid confusion and ensure that all important items are covered. An *order of business* should be given to the presiding officer to help prepare the agenda. The order of business includes the committees that are ready to report and the unfinished business from the last meeting.

An *agenda* is a list of the specific items under each order of business that the presiding officer will present to the membership. The secretary can prepare or assist the president in preparing the agenda. The agenda enables members to know in advance when each item of business will be considered.

Some organizations may have an established order of business in their rules. A recognized pattern for the order of business follows:

1. Reading and approval of minutes

2. Reports of officers, boards, and standing committees

3. Reports of special committees

4. Unfinished business

5. New business

6. Announcements

Each organization decides where it will insert other topics, such as roll call, payment of bills, correspondence, initiations, and inductions. If correspondence requires action by the assembly, it is read under new business and acted upon at that time.

Presiding

In the absence of the president or vice-president, the secretary calls the meeting to order and presides until a temporary chair, or a *chair pro tem*, is elected. The secretary should be familiar with the procedures for calling a meeting to order and presiding over the election of the chair pro tem.

Taking Notes

The secretary should have an outline of the items to be presented and copies of reports before the meeting begins. A list of the members should be on hand to check the names of those present or absent. The secretary should note those who arrive late and those who leave early, since an important issue may hinge on whether or not a certain member was present.

Secretaries should be sure to record the exact wording of motions. If a motion was not heard or understood, the secretary should interrupt the proceedings to get the exact wording. Secretaries also should note the length of the discussion and how the vote was taken. If business is left unfinished, secretaries should be sure to note the items that must be taken up at the next meeting.

The secretary should take notes that are accurate and thorough. These complete notes will help in writing the *minutes* that will be read at the next meeting. While notes are taken in depth, minutes are written in summary. It is always a good idea to transcribe the notes as soon as possible, while they are still fresh. It is also a good idea to hold on to the complete meeting notes until after the minutes have been approved.

The Secretary's Book

The secretary's book is the property of the organization. It should contain copies of the constitution, bylaws, standing rules, policies, procedures, current membership list, and committee lists. Copies of all minutes also should be included, in consecutive order. Written reports should be attached to the minutes or placed in a file. For ease of reference, it is helpful to keep meeting notes together and to number the pages to correspond with agenda items.

Other Duties

Secretaries may be responsible for a number of other duties. These duties may include sending out notice of meetings to the membership; providing paper for voting at meetings; furnishing committees with necessary documents; notifying officers, committee members, and delegates of their election or appointment; and following up on all action after the meeting.

Secretaries also may be responsible for conducting the correspondence of the organization. In some cases, a separate officer is elected or appointed to handle correspondence.

Another duty of the secretary is to make sure that the bylaws are correctly typed. The secretary should make necessary corrections in the numbering of articles, sections, or other subdivisions of the bylaws after they have been amended.

If a vote must be conducted by mail, the secretary should furnish the officials in charge of issuing the ballot with a list of the names and mailing addresses of all persons entitled to vote.

The Minutes

One of the most important responsibilities of the secretary is to prepare and present the minutes of each meeting. The minutes, prepared from the secretary's notes, are the official record of what transpired at the organization's meetings.

Minutes of a regular meeting are usually approved by general consent. However, a member may move that the minutes be approved as read. Minutes of a special meeting are read and approved at the next regular meeting. Minutes may be corrected whenever the error is noticed, even if it is months later. A member noticing the error can move to "amend something previously adopted." Only those who were present at a meeting can approve the minutes of that meeting.

Minutes for certain kinds of meetings may require special treatment. For example, the minutes of a convention usually are approved by the board or a special committee. Minutes of a board meeting may not be open for inspection by members unless the board grants permission; the board may instruct the secretary to give a summary of board actions at a regular meeting of the organization, however. The minutes of an executive session are read and acted upon only in the executive session. Finally, minutes generally are not kept in a small committee. The chair generally keeps complete notes of the proceedings, including options expressed, information gathered, and action taken.

There are a number of guidelines for most effectively keeping and presenting the minutes.

Format

The format of minutes varies with different organizations. However, minutes always are a brief summary of the proceedings of a meeting. They should be concise and sufficiently clear to be understood by a person not present at the meeting.

Minutes are evidence of what transpired at a meeting. After the reading and approval of the minutes, they become the official record of the transactions of the group. Therefore, the tone of the minutes should be impartial. Secretaries should be careful to avoid any personal comment. Members should be referred to by their titles, if any, or by their surnames.

Content

Minutes follow a regular order. The advantage to consistency is that members who are looking for information can find it easily.

The first paragraph of the minutes should specify the kind of meeting (regular, special, annual, adjourned); the name of the organization; the place, date, and hour; who was presiding and who was acting as secretary; attendance (by roll call, sign in, observation); and whether the minutes of the previous meeting were read and approved or mailed.

The body of the minutes should contain a separate paragraph for each subject. Some of the subjects that might be included in the body are

- Treasurer's report (read for information)

- Bills approved for payment

- Correspondence (read for information; if correspondence requires action, it should be read under new business)

- Condensed committee reports (entire reports may be attached)

It is often helpful to have a separate paragraph of the minutes for business transactions. Each paragraph should include the exact wording of the motion; the name of the person who made the motion; how the motion was acted upon or disposed of; and how the vote on the motion was taken. If a vote was counted, the minutes should include the number of votes for and against the motion.

Other items to be recorded in the minutes include:

- Names of persons appointed to committees

- All required notices

- Important announcements

- Names and subjects of speakers or participants at any program following the business

- Time of adjournment

- Secretary's signature

Common Mistakes in Preparing Minutes

There are a number of common errors that occur when secretaries are preparing the minutes of a meeting. One common error is the failure to show the complete wording of a motion. For example, poorly prepared minutes might read: "Mr. Johnson presented a resolution and moved its adoption. After amendment it was adopted as amended." A resolution is a substantive part of a motion. It should be recorded in the minutes as read by the member, and any amendments should be noted.

Another common mistake is the failure to show precise action taken on each motion made. The wording should clearly indicate how the motion was amended, if it was referred to a certain committee, or if it was postponed to the next meeting.

Still another common error is the failure to record important rulings. When a point of order is made, the chair makes a ruling that should be included in the minutes.

The last common mistake when preparing minutes is the failure to include complete, signed copies of all written reports presented at a meeting. Such items should be attached as numbered exhibits and legally made part of the minutes. References within the body of the minutes should state that such reports are attached.

Reading and Approval of Minutes

In organizations that hold weekly or monthly meetings, the minutes of the last meeting are the first item of business. Reading the minutes helps refresh the memories of those who were present and informs anyone who was absent.

The presiding officer calls upon the secretary to read the minutes. The secretary customarily rises to read them and remains standing while the president asks for corrections. If there are no corrections, the chair states that the minutes are approved as read. If there are corrections, the secretary makes the corrections in the margin.

Minutes are never rewritten after they have been read and corrected. If an error is pointed out and disputed, the secretary can refer to the notes or the presiding officer can take a vote to determine whether a mistake has been made. After the corrections have been completed, the president states that the minutes are approved as corrected. (A member also may move that the minutes be approved as corrected.) After approval, the secretary writes the word *approved* with the date, and signs or initials the minutes. The presiding officer may countersign.

In some organizations, the minutes are reproduced and sent to the members shortly after the meeting. This gives each member the information and the opportunity to correct any errors. If the minutes are mailed to the members, corrections can be made at the next meeting.

Dispensed Minutes

It may be necessary to dispense with the reading of the minutes. A motion can be made to dispense with the reading. This motion must be seconded. It is not debatable but can be amended. It requires a majority vote. If the presiding officer knows in advance that business must be attended to first, the presiding officer can say, "If there is no objection, the minutes will not be read at this time." He or she then waits and says, "Hearing no objection, the minutes will not be read." The reading of the minutes may be postponed to any later time during the meeting. If the minutes are not read at a given meeting, they must be read at the following meeting before the reading of the later minutes.

The reading of minutes should never be dispensed with unless a provision is made for correcting them.

Minute-Approving Committees

In order to save the time of reading lengthy minutes, a committee can be appointed or elected to approve the minutes. The committee has the responsibility for reading, correcting, and certifying the approval of the minutes. It is often a good idea to establish such a committee if the organization meets less than quarterly. Minutes should be approved by a committee when there is a different representation of delegates at the next meeting. A group of delegates cannot approve the minutes of a meeting they did not attend.

If the minutes will be approved by committee, committee members take their own notes at each meeting to serve as a check on the secretary's minutes. At the close of the meeting, the secretary sends a rough draft of the minutes to each committee member. The members check the minutes, make any necessary corrections, and sign and return them. The secretary makes the final draft of the minutes when all copies have been received. The secretary signs the minutes and adds "Approved by committee," listing the names of the committee members.

At the next meeting, the presiding officer states that the minutes have been approved by committee. However, a member can make a motion to have the minutes read.

Chapter 4

The Members

Amember of an organization has associational rights. These rights differ in each organization according to how they are provided for in the bylaws of the organization. To assert rights, a member must choose the proper time and follow the proper procedure.

Unless otherwise stated in the bylaws, members usually are responsible for the approval of matters pertaining to the policies, program, budget, and election of the officers and directors.

Since all members are seldom present at every meeting, it is necessary to allow a certain proportion of the membership to transact the business of the organization. This proportion of the membership is called the *quorum*. A quorum is the minimum number of voting members who must be present at a meeting in order for business to be legally transacted. A quorum always refers to the number present and not to the number actually voting. The number which constitutes a quorum should be provided for in the bylaws.

Duties of the Members

Members of any organization have special duties. Specific duties are spelled out by the organization's bylaws. However, some general duties are required of members of any body.

The first general duty of any member is to be familiar with the rules and customs of the organization. Members should keep the goals of the organization in mind. They should always follow the organization's guidelines for achieving those goals. If there are goals or guidelines that seem counterproductive, an informed member will know the organization's policies for making constructive changes.

Any time the organization convenes, members are responsible for keeping meetings running smoothly. Members always should pay close attention to speakers and to the business at hand. Remarks should be confined to the question before the assembly. Members should address all remarks to and through the presiding officer —not to other members.

A fundamental understanding of parliamentary procedure is very helpful to all members of an organization. Parliamentary procedure not only governs the mechanics of a meeting, it also ensures that members' rights are upheld. Every member should know the basic steps in presenting a motion. Every member also should know some of the most helpful motions—such as those that allow a member to ask questions about the debate.

Members also have a general duty to abstain from making remarks outside a meeting that might in any way interfere with the work being done by an officer or committee. Basically, members should make sure that their actions and remarks further the objectives of the organization.

Rights of the Members

Parliamentary law is built on rights: rights of the majority, rights of the minority, rights of individuals, and rights of absentees. Every member is responsible for seeing that these rights are respected.

When a person joins an organization, she or he acquires certain rights that are spelled out in the bylaws. There are also some fundamental rights.

Members have the right to receive notice of when meetings will be held and to attend those meetings. They also have the right to expect that meetings will begin on time and be properly conducted.

At any meeting, members have the right to explain or discuss motions that they present. Similarly, they have the right to discuss motions presented by others. Members have the right to speak without interruption, subject to the rules applicable to all members of the organization. They also have the right to request additional information from the presiding officer or to ask for an explanation of any pending question that is not understood.

Parliamentary procedure allows for some special cases in discussion. For example, if a motion contains two or more distinct propositions, each of which is capable of standing alone, members can ask to have the question divided. If the presiding officer has reached a decision that at least two members disagree with, the members have the right to appeal the decision of the chair. The members also have the right to raise a point of order when the presiding officer does not notice a mistake or omission.

Generally, all members have the right to nominate and to be nominated for office. They also have the right to vote or to abstain from voting—although members who do not vote have the effect of silently voting with the prevailing side. Members should vote for themselves when they are candidates for office. They also have the right to serve on committees.

Some other rights of members include:

- The right to resign if all obligations to the organization have been fulfilled

- The right to have a hearing before expulsion or other penalty

- The right to inspect official records of the organization in the presence of an officer

- The right to insist on enforcement of the rules of the organization

Regulations

In any meeting, with the rights of membership come certain procedural responsibilities. Members can be ruled *out of order* when they do not live up to those responsibilities.

A member can be ruled out of order for the following reasons:

1. Addressing another member instead of the chair in a debate.

2. Using the names of members in debate.

3. Failing to confine remarks to the merits of the pending question.

4. Persisting in speaking on irrelevant matters.

5. Making a motion and then speaking against it.

6. Speaking without first having risen, addressed the chair, and obtained the floor.

7. Speaking longer than permitted by the rules of the body.

8. Stating in debate that another's statement is false. (It is only acceptable to say that another is mistaken.)

9. Disturbing the assembly, such as by whispering or walking across the room.

Parliamentary Pointers for the Members

A member who is better informed will participate more confidently in debate and will be better respected by other members. A few pointers will help any member feel and sound in command of parliamentary procedure.

Parliamentary Phrases

How something is phrased often separates the savvy member from the one who is uncertain about parliamentary procedure.

When addressing the chair, any of the following are acceptable:

- Madam President—Mr. President

- Mr. Chair—Madam Chair

- Madam Moderator—Mr. Moderator

The correct way to begin a motion is with the words "I move that"—not "I motion that" or "I make a motion to." Motions always should be stated in the affirmative. It often is possible to express a negative idea in affirmative words. For example, "I move that we do not solicit funds for the convention" uses negative wording and is objectionable. The motion could be phrased, "I move that the funds for the convention be unsolicited."

The correct phrasing for a number of helpful parliamentary procedures is listed in Table 3.1.

Table 3.1

Parliamentary Phrases for the Members

Motions

- I move to amend the motion by . . . .

- I speak in favor of the motion . . . .

- I speak in opposition to the motion . . . .

- I object to the consideration of the motion (*or* resolution).

- I move to suspend the rules to take up . . . .

Voting

- Is there a quorum present?

- Division. *or* I call for a counted vote.

Debate

- I rise to a point of information.

- I rise to a parliamentary inquiry.

- I rise to a point of order.

- I appeal from the decision of the chair.

- Madam (*or* Mr.) President, will the member yield for a question?

Who May Speak

The first person who rises and asks for recognition when no member has the floor is entitled to be recognized. When two or more members rise to claim the floor, the member who rose and addressed the chair first is entitled to be recognized. When several members seek recognition at the same time, three basic rules help decide which member should be recognized.

First, preference is given to the proposer of a motion or to the committee chair who has presented a report. The person who made the motion is allowed to speak first to the motion. The person who made the report should be allowed to speak first to the committee's recommendations.

Second, a member who has not spoken has prior claim over one who has already discussed the question. This insures that as many views as possible are aired during every debate.

Third, debate should alternate between proponents and opponents of a motion. The chair may inquire which position a member will present.

In some cases, members may wish to interrupt speakers. Parliamentary procedure includes several motions that enable a member to interrupt debate. Such motions include:

- Point of order

- Question of privilege

- Point of no quorum

- Call for the orders of the day

- Appeal from the decision of the chair

- Parliamentary inquiry

- Question of information

- Give notice of information

- Objection to the consideration of a question
- Motion to divide a motion

Although this discussion has addressed when a member may speak, parliamentary procedure also addresses members who do not speak. Members who remain silent when presumably aware that they have been named to a duty are regarded as accepting that duty. They thereby place themselves under the same obligations as if they had accepted verbally.

Change of Vote

Members are permitted to change their votes. Change of vote is acceptable when the vote is taken by show of hands, voice, roll call, or standing. With a written ballot, change of vote is not possible, since there is no way to show how the member voted the first time.

To change a vote, a member might say the following: "I ask permission to change my vote from *Aye* to *No*." If no one objects when asked by the presiding officer, permission is granted. If someone objects—simply by calling out "Objection"—the member may move that he or she be permitted to change the vote. The motion must be seconded, and a majority vote is required to approve the change.

Members may change their votes only between the time they vote and the time the chair announces the result. When the chair says "The motion is carried" or "The motion is defeated," members lose the chance to change their votes without the permission of the assembly.

Chapter 5

Motions

Business is transacted in a meeting by way of motions. A member makes a proposal that is accepted or rejected. The members of the assembly may wish to defer consideration of the subject, or they may be willing to accept it with certain modifications.

Kinds of Motions

There are two kinds of motions: *primary* (or *main*) and *secondary*. The primary motion is the main motion—the proposal or proposition. If the main motion is accepted, it commits the assembly to take action. The main motion has implications beyond the present meeting.

Motions are classified in the following ways:

  I. Primary Motions
      A. Original
      B. Specific Main Motions
 II. Secondary Motions
      A. Subsidiary
      B. Privileged
      C. Incidental

The primary motion—main motion—brings business before the assembly. A secondary motion is a procedural motion that is made and considered while the main motion is on the floor. When a secondary motion is made, it becomes the immediately pending question, while the main motion remains pending. Certain secondary motions take priority over others. It is possible to have more than one secondary motion pending at the same time that the main motion is pending.

Main Motions

A main motion is a proposal that brings business before the assembly. The proposal is a member's request that something be done or that a statement express the sense, opinion, or wish of the assembly. As a general rule, a main motion is stated in the affirmative. It should be clear, definite, and brief. A long or complicated motion should be submitted in writing.

Parliamentary procedure governs how a motion should be presented and when it is in order. A main motion requires recognition by the chair, requires a second, is debatable, and is amendable. A main motion is not in order when another member has the floor. It yields to any subsidiary, privileged, or applicable incidental motion.

A main motion usually requires a majority vote. Exceptions to this rule include when the bylaws of the organization require a greater vote, when adoption would suspend a rule of order or a parliamentary right, or when adoption would rescind or amend something previously adopted. A main motion may be reconsidered by the assembly.

All subsidiary and privileged motions can be made while the main motion is pending. Other applicable incidental motions can be made, for example, division of the question, to consider seriatim (consider the proposition paragraph by paragraph), to withdraw, and to object to the consideration of an original main motion.

Specific main motions are motions that are incidental to or relate to the business of the assembly or to its past or future action. They usually are made orally. Some examples of specific main motions include:

- To ratify emergency action taken at a meeting when no quorum was present

- To rescind an action or rule already adopted

- To adopt a recommendation that an officer or committee has been directed to make

- To take a motion laid on the table from the table

- To amend something previously adopted

A member may object to the consideration of an original main motion, but it is not in order to object to the consideration of an incidental main motion.

Resolutions

A *resolution* is a formally written main motion. It may be a formal statement of the opinions of the assembly.

The difference between a standard main motion and a resolution is that a main motion is proposed by the words "I move that . . . ." A resolution is proposed by the words "I move the adoption of the following resolution,

Resolved, That . . . ." A resolution presented by a committee or board does not require a second, but all other rules pertaining to a main motion apply.

A resolution may have a *preamble*. A preamble consists of one or more clauses, each beginning with the word *Whereas*. The preamble is a brief statement giving the background or reasons for the motion. It presents arguments for the resolution's adoption. The preamble should contain only clauses that contain little-known information or items of unusual importance, without which the resolution is likely to be misunderstood.

The correct format for a resolution is illustrated below. In the preamble, the word *Whereas* introduces each item. It is followed by a comma. The next word begins with a capital letter, and the phrase ends with a semicolon followed by the word *and*. The last *Whereas* closes with a semicolon followed by the words *therefore be it* or simply *be it*. The beginning resolving clause begins a new line.

Whereas, A . . . ; and
Whereas, The . . .; therefore be it
Resolved, That [stating action to be taken]; and
Resolved, That [stating further action to be taken].

Each resolving clause in a resolution is voted on separately, as each is a primary motion. Each clause may be debated, amended, referred, postponed, or laid on the table. After the resolving clauses have been voted upon, the preamble is then put to a vote. Depending on the disposition of the resolving clauses, the preamble may be amended.

Courtesy Resolution

A committee is often charged with the duty of drafting and presenting to the assembly a *courtesy resolution*. Ordinarily, courtesy resolutions express the appreciation of an assembly or convention to those who arranged accommodations or rendered service. No opposing vote is taken on a courtesy resolution.

Subsidiary Motions

Subsidiary motions assist in treating or disposing of the main motion or other motions. They are used to modify, delay action on, or dispose of the pending motion. When a subsidiary motion is stated by the chair, it supersedes a pending motion of lower rank and becomes the immediately pending question.

Certain subsidiary motions may be applied to others. For example, a motion to amend may be amended, referred to a committee, or postponed. Debate on an amendment may be limited or extended by subsidiary motion.

Subsidiary motions, their purpose, and their application are discussed in depth in the Appendix "Handbook of Useful Motions," beginning on page 117.

Precedence of Motions

Before a subject can be considered, it must be brought before the assembly in the form of a motion or proposition. Only one main motion can be considered at a time. After the main motion has been stated by the chair, it must be adopted or rejected by the assembly, or the assembly must take some other action to dispose of it before any other subject can be brought up.

The consideration of a main motion may involve a number of secondary motions. Secondary motions enable an assembly to arrive at the general will of the members on a number of questions. The presiding officer is responsible for recognizing a secondary motion, its purpose, and its rank. The presiding officer should ensure that motions are handled in their proper order of precedence. Table 5.1 lists the various kinds of motions and shows their precedence.

Table 5.1

Table of Motions

	Can Interrupt Speaker	Requires Second	Debatable	Amendable	Vote Required	Can Be Reconsidered
Privileged Motions						
Fix the time to which to adjourn	no	yes	no	yes	majority	yes
Adjourn (unqualified)	no	yes	no	no	majority	no
Take a recess	no	yes	no	yes	majority	no
Question of privilege	yes	no	no	no	●	no
Orders of the day	yes	no	no	no	●	no
Subsidiary Motions						
Lay on the table (temporarily)	no	yes	no	no	majority	no
Previous question (stop debate)	no	yes	no	no	2/3	yes
Limit or extend debate	no	yes	no	yes	2/3	yes
Postpone to certain time	no	yes	yes	yes	majority	yes

	Can Interrupt Speaker	Requires Second	Debatable	Amendable	Vote Required	Can Be Reconsidered
Refer to committee	no	yes	yes	yes	majority	yes
Amend	no	yes	yes	yes	majority	yes
Postpone indefinitely	no	yes	yes	no	majority	aff. vote only
Main Motion	no	yes	yes	yes	majority	yes
Specific Main Motions						
Reconsider	no	yes	yes*	no	majority	no
Ratify	no	yes	yes	yes	majority	yes
Rescind	no	yes	yes	yes	(1)	neg. vote only
Take from the table	no	yes	no	no	majority	no
Discharge committee	no	yes	yes	yes	2/3	neg. vote only
Amend something previously adopted	no	yes	yes	yes	(1)	neg. vote only

* Except when the motion to be reconsidered is debatable.

● Chair usually decides. Majority if put to vote.

(1) Requires a two-thirds vote when applied to constitution, bylaws, or special rules. Requires a majority vote when notice is given at a previous meeting, or a majority vote of the entire membership without notice.

(2) If not granted by general consent, can be moved by person requesting permission.

(3) Yes, if motion made by person requesting permission.

	Can Interrupt Speaker	Requires Second	Debatable	Amendable	Vote Required	Can Be Reconsidered
Incidental Motions (no rank)						
Point of order	yes	no	no	no	●	no
Appeal from the decision of chair	yes	yes	limited	no	majority	yes
Suspend the rules of order	no	yes	no	no	2/3	no
Suspend standing rules	no	yes	no	no	majority	no
Object to consideration	yes	no	no	no	2/3	neg. vote only
Division of a question (motion)	no	yes	no	yes	majority	no
Consider by paragraph (section)	no	yes	no	yes	majority	no
Division of assembly (vote)	yes	no	no	no	none	no
Close polls	no	yes	no	yes	2/3	no

	Can Interrupt Speaker	Requires Second	Debatable	Amendable	Vote Required	Can Be Reconsidered
Reopen polls	no	yes	no	yes	majority	neg. vote only
Close nominations	no	yes	no	yes	2/3	no
Reopen nominations	no	yes	no	yes	majority	neg. vote only
Parliamentary inquiry	yes	no	no	no	none	no
Request for information	yes	no	no	no	none	no
Excused for duty	no	yes	yes	yes	majority	neg. vote only
Withdraw a motion	(1)	(2)	no	no	majority	neg. vote only
Create a blank	no	yes	no	no	majority	no
Fill a blank	no	no	yes	no	majority	yes
Request to read a paper	(1)	(2)	no	no	majority	yes
Motions relating to voting	no	yes	no	yes	majority	no

* Except when the motion to be reconsidered is debatable.
● Chair usually decides. Majority if put to vote.
(1) Requires a two-thirds vote when applied to constitution, bylaws, or special rules. Requires a majority vote when notice is given at a previous meeting, or a majority vote of the entire membership without notice.
(2) If not granted by general consent, can be moved by person requesting permission.
(3) Yes, if motion made by person requesting permission.

Chapter 6

Nominations
and Elections

The method of nominating and electing officers should be specified in the bylaws of the organization. If no method is prescribed in the bylaws, a member may move that nominations be made by the chair, by a committee, by ballot, or that they be taken from the floor.

A *nomination* is a proposal that a certain position be filled. It is an assurance that the nominee will serve in the specified office if elected. One who seeks an office is a *candidate*. When the candidate's name is put up for nomination, he or she is then a *nominee*.

Nominations

A member cannot nominate more than one person for an office until all members have had an opportunity to nominate someone. A nomination does not require a second.

Nominations cannot be amended; however, a nominating speech may be given.

No motion is necessary to close nominations. The chair simply declares that nominations are closed. However, if a motion is made to close nominations, the motion requires a two-thirds vote. Nominations may be reopened by a majority vote.

If a person is nominated and unable or unwilling to serve, he or she should decline immediately. The same person can be nominated for more than one office. However, if elected to more than one office, the person must decide in which office she or he will serve. If the person is absent from the actual election, the assembly must decide which office that person will fill.

Nominations by the Chair

One nominating procedure is nomination by the chair. In this method, the presiding officer puts forth nominees for the offices that are to be filled. The assembly then votes on the chair's nominees.

Nominations by Committee

In an election of officers, nominations usually are made by a *nominating committee*. Usually the bylaws of the organization specify if the committee is elected or appointed. The committee may be a standing committee, or it may be a special committee elected in advance of the officer election.

Members on the nominating committee should represent the various interest groups in the organization. The president should have no part in the selection of the committee, nor be an ex-officio member of it.

The nominating committee members should be familiar with the membership and the organization bylaws that describe the nominating procedures. By studying the needs of the organization, the committee can prepare a list of potential officers who can work together well and represent different groups within the organization. Several questions should be considered in the committee meeting:

1. Does the person being considered believe in the objectives of the organization?

2. Does the person have the time to devote to the duties of the office?

3. Does the person have a good relationship with others in the organization?

4. What has been the past performance of the person?

When preparing to select nominees, the nominating committee should request a current membership list and an attendance record from the secretary of the organization. Members of the organization may suggest names of prospective nominees for the committee's review. A member of the nominating committee may be considered as a candidate. It is not necessary for the member to resign from the committee.

When the committee agrees on a prospective candidate, the candidate should be contacted while the committee is still in session to make sure she or he will serve if nominated and elected. No prospective candidate should be contacted by an individual committee member prior to the committee meeting. Once selected and contacted, the committee must have the candidate's agreement to serve before that person's name is included in the committee report. Some organizations require that such an agreement be signed before an individual is included as a candidate.

The number of nominees for each office depends on the bylaws of the organization. Unless the bylaws state otherwise, the committee is only required to submit one candidate for each office to be filled. Selection of a candidate should be by majority vote.

The information discussed in committee is confidential. The nominating committee should make every effort to weigh the qualifications and responsibilities of each person and of the office. The committee's candidate should be the individual best suited to the position.

Committee Report

After a majority of the committee has agreed on the nominees, a report is made and signed by all members who agree on it. The report is read to the assembly by the committee chair at the request of the presiding officer. It is then given to the presiding officer or the secretary. The report is not accepted or adopted by the members.

After the report has been read, the committee is automatically discharged. It can be recalled if a nominee withdraws (or declines) before the election. If the committee's nominee is elected and then resigns, the vacancy is filled by the prescribed method in the bylaws.

Nominations by Ballot

Nominations by ballot usually are managed by the nominating committee. The nominating committee prepares a ballot containing the names of the nominees and space for nominations from the floor or write-in candidates. The ballot is given to each voting member. The chair then instructs the members how to mark and fold the ballot.

When the balloting is completed, the chair directs the *tellers* to collect the ballots. Tellers are responsible for ensuring that the balloting proceeds smoothly and that no member votes more than once. Because of this, ballots should not simply be passed to the center isle. When only voters are present, members can remain in their seats and drop their ballots into a receptacle passed by one teller and checked by another teller. An alternative method is to have members go to a central ballot box and deposit their ballots. Ballots also can be handed to a teller, who then deposits them in a central box.

Nominations from the Floor

The procedure for taking nominations from the floor is fairly simple. The presiding officer states that nominations are in order for a particular office. It is then in order for any member to make a nomination for the office. Generally, when the chair calls for nominations from the floor, a member need not rise and be recognized by the chair. However, in a large meeting or a convention, members should rise.

When making a nomination, the member should state, "I nominate Member Alvarez." The chair then repeats the nomination ("Member Alvarez has been nominated") and asks for further nominations. When all nominations have been made, the chair closes the nominations. A motion is not necessary; however, if a member does move to close nominations, the motion must be seconded and requires a two-thirds vote.

It is possible to reopen nominations after they have been closed. The member should rise, wait for recognition by the chair, and then state, "I move that nominations be reopened for the office of . . . ." The motion must be seconded. It is not debatable, but it may be amended. The chair then calls for a voice vote to reopen the nominations. If the vote is in the affirmative, the chair calls for further nominations.

After nominations have been closed, voting for that office takes place, or nominations for the next office can be called for by the chair.

Elections

Each organization should adopt the method of electing officers best suited to the organization. This method should be spelled out in the bylaws, and all required formalities should be observed. For example, if the bylaws require an election to be by ballot, a motion to dispense with the ballot is illegal. Similarly, the secretary may be instructed to cast the elective ballot only if provided for in the bylaws.

When only one candidate is nominated for an office, provision should be included for a simple method of election. Generally, if a candidate is unopposed and the bylaws do not require election to be by ballot, the chair may call for a voice vote.

When it appears that everyone has voted, the chair closes the polls. A majority vote is required to elect a nominee to office. A single vote may be considered a majority vote if it is the only vote cast. A *plurality vote* (largest number of votes cast) does not elect, unless provided for in the bylaws or by a specially adopted rule.

An election becomes final immediately if the candidate is present and did not decline the nomination. If the candidate is absent and has not consented to the nomination, the election becomes final when she or he is notified of the election and does not decline.

Tellers

In addition to distributing, collecting, and counting ballots, tellers are appointed by the chair to report the vote. It is the tellers' responsibility to see that no member votes more than once. The number of tellers varies with the number of voters. (A minimum of two or three is advised.) Tellers are chosen for accuracy and dependability. They should not be personally involved in the election.

Tellers' Procedure

Tellers distribute ballots to those entitled to vote in the election. After the presiding officer declares the voting closed, the ballots are collected and then counted. The counting preferably takes place in another room. When counting the ballots, tellers should make certain that the number of ballots is equal to or less than the number of eligible voters.

Tally sheets should be used to count the votes. They should be prepared by the tellers when nominations are complete. A minimum of four tellers is advisable, so that one teller can serve as a check on the other. If there are four tellers, the first teller opens the ballot, the second teller reads the ballot aloud, and the third and fourth tellers mark their tally sheets.

Tally sheets are marked with vertical lines in groups of four, with a fifth mark going diagonally across the four vertical lines. When a teller makes the fifth mark, he or she calls out "Tally." The other tellers should be in agreement. If they do not agree, they should recheck the last five ballots.

When tallying votes, blank ballots are not counted. Misspelled words or names are counted if the meaning is clear. Illegal votes are recorded separately. When all votes have been tallied, the tellers' report is compiled in duplicate (see Figure 6.1 for sample tellers' report). The tally sheets are sealed in an envelope. Tally sheets should be retained until there is no possibility of them being required again; they should then be destroyed.

The tellers return to the assembly and present their report when called upon. The chair of the tellers reads the report and then presents it to the president, who announces the results. Because votes are confidential, tellers may not divulge the vote of anyone whose ballot they recognized.

Figure 6.1

Sample Tellers' Report

1. The number eligible to vote _____

2. The number of votes cast _____

3. The number of votes necessary to elect _____

4. The number of votes received by each candidate

   Candidate   Number of Votes
   _____   _____

   _____   _____

   _____   _____

   _____   _____

5. Illegal votes _____

Chapter 7

Bylaws and Standing Rules

The *bylaws* of an organization are the rules adopted by the members to regulate and manage the organization's business and to set forth the rights and duties of its members. They also define the specific duties and responsibilities of directors and elected officers. The bylaws of membership organizations vary, depending on the objectives of the organization.

Bylaws have a direct bearing on the rights of members within an organization. Every member should be given a copy of the bylaws to study. When a member joins an organization, that member agrees to abide by its bylaws.

Content of Bylaws

Everything relating to a subject should be placed in the same or adjacent article of the bylaws. Each article may have several subdivisions. Nothing in the bylaws should conflict with other articles.

Expressions used in bylaws should be clear. For example, under an article on officers, if the term of office is stated as "one year," at the end of one year the term expires, whether or not a successor has been elected. However, by using the expression "one year and/or until the successor is elected," the officer holds over until the successor is elected. If *or* is used, the organization has a right to declare an office vacant by the same vote required to rescind any action taken. If *and* is used, the organization cannot vacate an office.

Bylaws are prepared by a committee. It is the committee's function to make certain that the bylaw provisions do not conflict with the actual operating procedures and objectives of the organization. A bylaws committee should include the persons interested, as well as those who are likely to spend much time in discussing the bylaws. After the large committee has had one or two meetings on the subject and has come to an agreement, it should appoint a subcommittee of two or three persons to actually write the bylaws.

Structure of Bylaws

Bylaws provide the legal framework within which the organization functions. Bylaws are divided into *articles* assigned with Roman numerals. Each article is subdivided into *sections*, or paragraphs, in which Arabic numerals are assigned. By convention, the word *article* should be placed in the center of the page and the word *section* to the left of the page.

The standard pattern for bylaws is illustrated in Figure 7.1. Usually the name of the organization is the first article, the object or purpose of the organization is the second article, and subsequent articles have to do with membership, finances, officers, meetings, and such. It is helpful to have an article that deals with the bylaws themselves, so that members know the proper procedure for amendments.

Presenting the Bylaws

After the proposed bylaws have been examined by the bylaws committee, and no inconsistencies or ambiguities exist, they should be typed and circulated to the membership well in advance of the meeting at which they are to be voted on. Copies should be shown ahead of time to the parliamentarian and other legal advisors so that any legal or technical questions can be resolved.

At the voting meeting, the presiding officer calls on the bylaws committee to report. The committee chair says, "By direction of the committee, I move the adoption of the proposed bylaws." No second is necessary.

The bylaws then are read, one article or section at a time. Each article or section is then open to debate and amendment. When amendment of one section is complete, the next is considered.

After the last article has been completed, the chair asks for any further amendments. If there are any, they are considered. When all the amendments are complete, the chair asks for a vote on the adoption of the bylaws as amended. Normally, bylaws are adopted by a two-thirds vote. If bylaws are being adopted for the first time, only a majority vote is necessary. The vote may be taken by voice.

Amendments to Bylaws

After a period of time it may be necessary to amend portions of the bylaws. The motion to amend the bylaws is an incidental main motion. It is subject to the same rules as a main motion, except that the vote required for its adoption is specified in the bylaws. A proposed amendment may be amended by a majority vote.

A proposed amendment to the bylaws should be stated in language that, if adopted, may be incorporated directly into the bylaws. Some organizations provide that the proposed amendment be given to the bylaws committee for study. The committee then reports its recommendations to the voting members. When reporting, the committee should fully explain every section, and explain the changes that will result from the proposed change.

Amendment Procedures

Parliamentary procedure governs certain elements of amending bylaws. First, no amendment is in order that increases the modification of the article or rule to be amended. Second, in an amendment to strike out a sentence, paragraph, or section, the existing bylaw itself is not open to consideration, only the amendment to the bylaw.

Next, an amendment to the bylaws goes into effect immediately with the announcement of the vote adopting it, unless the motion to adopt provides that it become effective at a later time.

Fourth, to change the quorum provision in the bylaws, the proper procedure is to strike out and insert the new provision in one sentence and to vote on it as one question.

Finally, an amendment or motion to change the number of sections or paragraphs is not necessary. The secretary makes such corrections as they become necessary.

The procedure for amending the bylaws should be set forth in the bylaws. The power to amend the bylaws lies primarily with the membership as a whole. However, this power may be delegated to the board of directors, unless prohibited by the bylaws or articles of incorporation.

Revising Bylaws

When changes in the bylaws are extensive and scattered throughout, a substitution should be made with an entirely new set of bylaws. Amending bylaws by substitution is called a *revision*. The best method is to select a special committee for this purpose, or the bylaws committee may submit a revision.

A copy of the proposed revision with the date it will be considered and voted upon should be sent to each member in advance of the meeting. It is considered and voted upon under the same procedure that is followed for adopting the original bylaws. Each article is discussed and any amendments are acted upon at that time. Each amendment requires a majority vote. When there are no further amendments nor any further discussion, a counted standing vote is taken.

A revised set of bylaws becomes effective immediately after the vote adopting the new revision. However, it is possible to adopt a motion to provide that certain portions of the revised bylaws should not become effective until a specified time.

Standing Rules

An organization's *standing rules* usually relate to administrative details. Any adopted main motion which has continuing effects is a standing rule. It continues in force until it is rescinded. Examples of standing rules include: time for the meeting to begin; location of the meeting; policy concerning guests; and responsibilities for refreshments. Standing rules are adopted as the need arises at any business meeting. No previous notice is necessary.

Standing rules for a convention are not the same as the standing rules for the organization. A committee generally prepares the proposed rules that cover such subjects as seating of delegates and alternates, length of speeches, and privileges of nonvoting members. While these rules apply only to a particular convention, they may be held over to another convention with only slight changes.

After the convention rules committee reports, the rules may be debated or amended. A single member may ask for a separate vote on any individual rule. The rules usually are adopted as a whole by a two-thirds vote. During the convention, any standing rule can be suspended by a majority vote.

Figure 7.1

Basic Pattern for Bylaws

ARTICLE I

NAME

1. Give full, exact name, properly punctuated

2. Name should have some relationship to the purpose and function of the organization

3. Name should be clearly understood

ARTICLE II

OBJECT *or* PURPOSE

1. May be expressed in a single sentence

2. May be specified in a series of descriptive phrases set off by semicolons

3. Each statement should be clearly worked out so that it cannot be misinterpreted

4. Serves as the basic authority for future actions of the organization

ARTICLE III

MEMBERS

1. Classes of membership (active, associate, sustaining, firm, life, inactive, honorary, emeritus, family)

   a. Rights of each class (distinction between classes; limitations on number; family membership—can husband and wife have joint membership; age limit for children voting)

2. Qualifications for membership

   a. Limited to those in a certain geographical area?

   b. How are members admitted? (invitation, sponsor, credit rating, ethnic background, age, other)

3. Procedure for applying for membership

   a. Approved application? (what questions are included)

   b. Time schedule for handling applications (including time limitations for reaching a decision about applications)

4. Termination of membership

5. Rights of members (to hold office, participate in functions and activities)

6. Resignation of membership

7. Transfer of membership

8. Honorary members and officers

ARTICLE IV

FINANCES

1. Required dues and fees

2. Date payable (annually, quarterly)

3. Do fees and dues vary for different classes of membership?

4. Time and procedure for notifying members if they become delinquent in payment

5. Penalties for nonpayment

6. Date when member will be dropped for nonpayment

7. Does a delinquent member maintain voting rights?

8. Does the organization have the right and power to assess members additional sums on top of dues?

9. Fiscal year and membership year

10. Conference or convention expenses for officers

11. Bond for treasurer

12. Check authorization and endorsement (how many officers, which ones)

13. Audit

14. Budget (when presented)

ARTICLE V

OFFICERS

1. Title and number of officers

2. Qualifications

3. Term of office and powers of each officer

4. Duties of each officer (which duties will be handled by officers and which duties by committees)

5. Vacancies (how filled)

6. Appointed officers

7. Directors

   a. Term of office

   b. How elected

   c. How many

ARTICLE VI

NOMINATIONS and ELECTIONS

1. Nominating committee

   a. When appointed or elected?

   b. Number of terms a member may serve

c. Eligibility of members (from different regions?)

d. Duties

e. Required number of nominees for each office

f. Nominations from floor

g. When to report

h. Rules governing nominees

2. Elections

 a. When? (first order of business?)

 b. By ballot (procedure to follow if candidate does not receive a majority vote)

 c. By mail (describe procedure)

 d. By proxy (describe procedure)

 e. By voice if only one candidate, or chair declare the candidate elected

ARTICLE VII

MEETINGS

1. Kinds of meetings

 a. Regular (day on which meeting is held; the hour should be in the standing rules)

 b. Special (who may call a special meeting; how far in advance notice must be given; how members are notified)

 c. Annual (for the purpose of hearing annual reports, conducting elections; time, place, notice of meeting)

2. Quorum

ARTICLE VIII

(The title of this article may vary. Options include: Executive Committee; Board of Directors; Councils; Board of Governors; Board of Managers; Board of Trustees)

1. Composition (qualifications, term of office)

2. Powers

   a. Full power and authority over affairs of the organization (with certain exceptions)

   b. Does the board control the whole organization?

   c. Does the board have limited power to act for the organization between meetings?

   d. Specific powers (to elect their own officers, fill vacancies, discharge employees of the organization)

   e. Review and termination of memberships for cause

   f. Purchasing power, selling or lease of property.

3. Meetings of the board

   a. How often? (notice to be given)

   b. Right of an ordinary member to be informed of board activities

   c. Report to the membership

   d. How special meetings are called

   e. Do repeated absences constitute an automatic resignation?

   f. How are vacancies filled?

4. Quorum

ARTICLE IX

COMMITTEES

1. Standing committees listed by name (no other committees can be added without amending the bylaws; list all essential committees)

   a. Composition of the committee

   b. Vacancies, quorum

   c. Manner of selecting members for the committee

   d. Shall the president be an ex-officio member?

2. Special committees (ad hoc)

   a. How elected or appointed

   b. Duties and powers

ARTICLE X

(At this place other articles may be added. Suggested articles include: Conventions; Regions; Councils; Discipline; Seal or Emblem; Indemnification; Publications; Headquarters. Each should be in a separate article. There should be a separate article on Dissolution to meet the requirements of the IRS.)

(Next to the last ARTICLE)

PARLIAMENTARY AUTHORITY

(State the parliamentary authority that is to be the guide on all matters not covered by the organization's charter, bylaws, or standing rules.)

(Always the last ARTICLE)

AMENDMENTS TO BYLAWS

1. How changes are to be made (by committee, by individual member of the organization)

2. Notice of the amendment

   a. In writing (form in which proposed amendments are to be stated)

   b. How far in advance (required notice to all members; notice given at *a* previous meeting is not the same as *the* previous meeting)

3. Procedure for approving an amendment

4. Vote required (voice, ballot, mail)

5. Emergency procedures (disaster preventing the holding of a convention or national catastrophe)

Part Two

Committees and Boards

How to Be an Effective Participant

Chapter 8

Committees

A *committee* is a small group of one or more persons appointed or elected by an organization. The purpose of a committee is to consider, to investigate relevant matters, to report facts or findings to the assembly, or to take action.

Through committees, the activities of an organization are accomplished. Committees differ widely as to the duties or powers entrusted to them. They promote the official programs of the organization and undertake the various technical aspects of efficient club work.

Committees can make many contributions to an organization. If properly selected and oriented, committees can relieve officials of many of the details of carrying on the activities of the organization. Committees permit wider participation of an organization's members, and a greater sense of commitment to the organization. Through their contacts outside the organization, committee members can provide means to accomplish the goals of the organization. Finally, committees also provide an excellent training ground for new leaders.

This part of *Meetings: Rules & Procedures* is designed to help readers use parliamentary procedure to most effectively participate in ordinary committees and in boards, both as officers and as members of an organization.

Kinds of Committees

Committees are divided into two classes. *Ordinary committees* are usually appointed to study, deliberate, investigate, or work for the organization. They are further subdivided into *standing* or *special* committees. Standing committees are listed in the bylaws of the organization, while special committees are elected or appointed when special needs arise.

The second class of committees is *boards*. Boards usually consist of elected representatives of the organization. The members usually are known as directors, the cabinet, the council, managers, trustees, or governors of the organization. Because the roles and operations of boards are specialized, their workings are treated in a separate chapter.

Committee Functions

Committees must know what their exact functions are. The secretary or presiding officer should give members specific instructions about their goals and responsibilities.

The preliminary information that committees should have includes the following:

- Name of committee

- Type of committee (standing or special)

- Purpose of committee, specific duties and responsibilities

- Names of chair and other members

- Time of reporting (monthly, year-end)

- Budget amount allowed

- Coordination with other committees (list special interest committees that may be working on matters related to the work of the committee; include chair's name, address, and phone number)

- Other materials and references that may be of value to the committee

Committee Size

The size of a committee depends on the task or purpose assigned to it. If the purpose of the committee requires wide representation, the committee could be larger. If the purpose of the committee is to address a relatively small task, the committee might consist of only three or four persons. The major reason for appointing a committee is the efficiency and flexibility of a smaller group. Size, therefore, should be determined by the minimum number of persons needed to accomplish the committee's purpose.

Selecting Committees

If a motion is made to refer a matter to a committee, the presiding officer should ask how the committee should be obtained. There are five methods of selecting committees: appointment by the chair; nomination by the chair; nomination from the floor; nomination by ballot; and as part of the motion naming the committee. After methods have been suggested by the members, the presiding officer calls a vote. The first method to receive a majority affirmative vote is used. If only one method for obtaining a committee is suggested, it is used without a vote unless an objection is raised.

If a committee member resigns after being elected or appointed, the vacancy must be filled by the same method used to originally establish the membership of the committee.

Appointment by the Chair

The presiding officer may appoint the members of a committee. This method is most often used. The members that are appointed are not subject to amendment or vote.

The first member named by the presiding officer is generally considered the chairperson of the committee. If the first appointee declines the position of chair, it is the duty of that person to call a meeting of the committee and act as temporary chair until the permanent chair is selected.

Nomination by the Chair

The presiding officer may nominate committee members. A vote is then taken on the group collectively.

Before the vote is taken, a member can move to amend the nominations by striking the names of certain members. If the amendment is adopted, the presiding officer nominates another to fill the vacancy. A majority vote elects the members of the committee.

Nomination from the Floor

Nominations for committee members may be made from the floor. A member need not be recognized by the chair to make a nomination, and no second is required. If more are nominated than are needed on the committee, the presiding officer calls for a vote on each nomination in order, and those who receive a majority vote are declared elected. If there are remaining nominees, they are not voted on.

If only three members are nominated for a committee requiring only three members, those persons are declared members of the committee without a vote, unless an objection is raised.

As Part of the Motion Naming the Committee

The member who makes the motion to refer a matter to committee may at the same time propose the members of the committee. This motion may be amended in any way.

Nomination by Ballot

Nominations for a committee can be made by ballot. Under this method, each voting member receives a ballot.

Each member writes a nominee's name on the ballot. If there are more nominees than are to be on the committee, a vote can be taken to elect the number required.

Conducting Committee Business

A committee has only the power granted to it by the bylaws of the organization or given to it by the assembly. The formalities of the general assembly generally are not observed in a small committee. Matters often are discussed before they are put to the members in the form of a motion. The committee chair usually leads the discussion. He or she does not need to leave the chair in order to make a motion. However, if a committee is large, the formal rules of the assembly should be observed.

Rules Governing Committees

In a committee, questions may be discussed before a motion is made. Members do not have to rise and address the chair before speaking or making a motion, and motions do not require a second. As part of this relative informality, there is no limit on the number of times a member may speak on a question. Similarly, motions to limit or close debate generally are not permitted.

A motion to reconsider a question may be made by any member, even after a vote has been taken. A member who was absent when a matter was voted on may move to a reconsideration.

Committee meetings usually are confidential. Only members of the committee have the right to attend committee deliberations. Others may attend only when invited or given permission to attend.

A committee may appoint a subcommittee from its own members. The subcommittee is responsible to the committee, and not to the assembly.

Agendas

An *agenda* is a plan for addressing business. In committees, an agenda is a valuable tool for keeping the purpose of the committee in mind and for making sure that the committee's business will be completed in a timely manner.

A committee agenda should include the committee's objectives for the year, or for the period that the committee will be in existence. The agenda also should include a list of projects that will be undertaken within that time frame.

One of the most important components of a committee agenda is deadlines. Each project should have a specific culmination date. Committee members should keep these dates in mind as they go about the business.

Committee Members

Committee members should be carefully selected. The more important the committee, the more care is required.

All committee members should be genuinely interested in the business of the committee. They also should be dependable, able to accept reponsibility, and work well with other members. Working well with others involves being a good listener, being fair-minded, and being able to abide by the decision of the group.

It also is important that committee members feel that their efforts make a difference. Committee work is one of the best opportunities for members of large organizations to make a genuine, visible contribution to the business of the organization.

In addition to the regular (elected or appointed) committee members, committees may find themselves working with ex-officio members and observers.

Ex-Officio Members

If the bylaws state that the president or another officer is to be an *ex-officio member* of a committee, that person must receive notice of the meetings. An officer is made an ex-officio member by virtue of the office. For example, the treasurer of an organization may be made an ex-officio member of the finance committee, or the parliamentarian may be an ex-officio member of the rules committee. Ex-officio members have the same rights as regular members, but they are not required to attend meetings and are not counted in determining a quorum (number of members that must be present in order to conduct business).

Observers

Although meetings of a committee may not be open to members of the organization, at times it may be convenient to open the meeting, in a limited way, to members who otherwise are not eligible to attend.

When a committee is to make a decision on an important matter, it is wise to give the members of the general assembly *observer status*. The members then receive notice of the meeting and the right to attend. They have no voting rights, but if permission is given they can have an opportunity to present their views on the subject.

The observer system can be used to bring in individuals who have special knowledge about a matter the committee is considering. However, only the committee members have the right to be present during the actual deliberation of the committee.

Discharging Committees

The assembly cannot consider a question that has been referred to committee without taking the question out of the committee's hands. Normally, the committee makes its report within a specified period of time and the committee is then automatically discharged.

However, if a committee fails to make its report promptly, if it is necessary to consider a question before the committee can make its report, or if a question is to be dropped, a motion to discharge the committee may be in order.

The motion to discharge a committee cannot be made when any other question is pending. Exceptions occur when a committee has made a partial report and there is a motion either to accept the report or to accept the report and continue the committee. A motion to discharge the committee may be made as an amendment and adopted by a majority vote.

If the committee has made no report, a member may give notice that at the next meeting a motion will be made to discharge the committee. This motion requires a second and is debatable.

The motion to discharge may be amended by instructing the committee to report instead of being discharged. If previous notice has been given, the motion requires a majority vote to discharge the committee. If no notice has been given, a two-thirds vote is required.

When a committee is discharged, the chair should give the secretary all the papers relative to the subject that was entrusted to the committee.

Chapter 9

The Committee Chair

The key factor in the success of any committee's work is its chairperson. The chair must be willing to give freely of time and talent. The chair should be someone able to lead the other committee members to a successful completion of their assigned task.

The Effective Committee Chair

The chair should define the objectives of the committee. With the help of the members, the chair can outline the year's work and delegate the responsibilities to the members in relation to their skills and interests.

The chair also must make the committee members feel that they are doing the job. The chair should resist the urge to do all of the work independently. He or she also should resist the urge to assume the credit for what the committee accomplishes. When everything has been completed, credit should be given to the entire committee.

An effective committee chair stimulates others to work, is patient, does not show favoritism, and does not overload key members of the committee.

Responsibilities of the Chair

The first responsibility of the committee chair is to have a clear knowledge of the job assigned. The chair should be able to explain the primary and the lesser goals to the members.

The committee chair is responsible for calling committee meetings to order. He or she should make sure that the time and place of meetings are convenient to all members, and he or she also should make sure that all members are notified in advance and briefed on the items to be discussed. Like a presiding officer, the committee chair should prepare an agenda before the meeting and call the meeting to order on time.

If a committee chair fails to call a meeting, any two of its members should call a meeting, unless the organization's bylaws state otherwise.

The chair should keep discussion under control, talking to the entire group and calling on everyone for possible solutions. The chair should make sure each speaker is heard and understood, and that no one dominates the discussion. If tasks have been assigned to individual members, the chair should keep up-to-date on the individuals' progress. Finally, the chair should try to keep conflicts between individuals to a minimum.

It is important for a committee chairperson to maintain a positive approach. It is often helpful to discuss why each problem has to be solved, in case committee members are uncertain about the issues. Solutions should be acceptable to all. This often means not rushing the discussion and taking time to consider alternatives.

When a solution has been reached, the chair should get a verbal commitment to the solution from each member of the committee. A commitment given in the presence of others is often more binding. In small committees, the chair acts as secretary by keeping informal notes of the discussion. Based on these notes, the chair should prepare a report of the committee's activities and solutions and present the report to the assembly as required.

Rules Regarding Committee Chairs

The committee chair cannot remove other members from the committee, for example, for not attending meetings, unless the chair appointed those members. However, the chair may ask members to resign from the committee.

If a committee chair resigns, a new chair usually is appointed by the authority that established the committee and authorized the chair. For example, if the chair was appointed by the president of the organization, the president should appoint a new chair. However, if a new chair is not appointed within a reasonable amount of time by the proper authority, the committee may elect its own chair.

Chapter 10

Ordinary Committees

There are two kinds of ordinary committees. Standing committees are provided for in the bylaws of an organization. Special committees are appointed or elected as special needs arise.

Standing Committees

The bylaws of an organization provide for *standing committees*. The number and kind of standing committees depend on the size and the activities of the organization. The members of a standing committee serve for a term corresponding to that of the officers. They continue their duties until their successors have been chosen. The chair of a committee usually is appointed by the president. The members are selected on the basis of their qualifications for the particular work of the committee.

Budget Committee

In most organizations, one of the most important standing committees is the *budget committee*. The budget committee works closely with all other committees to make sure that the financial resources of the organization are directed into the overall work of the organization.

The budget committee is responsible for preparing the budget of the organization. The budget should be based on the maximum needs of the overall program. In order to arrive at a fair and workable budget, the committee should review the estimated and actual expenses for at least two preceding years; examine and analyze the organization's financial policies; receive full information on the financial requirements of the year's activities from each officer and committee chair; and include all program plans that require expenditures. A sample budget form is provided in Figure 10.1.

The *income budget* is prepared first. All sources of income should be included:

- Dues (based on actual, not estimated, figures)

- Conservative estimate of income expected from other sources

- Funds to be collected from contributions to special projects

- Any previous balance from the budget (unless such money is to be set aside as a contingency fund)

- Special or dedicated funds for special projects (these must be kept separate from general funds)

The *estimated expenditures* are prepared next. They should be based on a sound distribution of available funds. The expense budget may be broken down into several major headings. An unallocated amount should be indicated so that new or emergency projects can be carried out.

Figure 10.1

Sample Budget

Estimated Income

Dues ⎯⎯ Members @ ⎯⎯⎯⎯⎯⎯   ⎯⎯⎯⎯⎯⎯

Other sources of income   ⎯⎯⎯⎯⎯⎯

⎯⎯⎯⎯⎯⎯

   Total anticipated income   ⎯⎯⎯⎯⎯⎯

   Unexpected from previous term   ⎯⎯⎯⎯⎯⎯

Total available for budgeting   ⎯⎯⎯⎯⎯⎯

Estimated Expenditures

Dues to parent organization
     ⎯⎯ members @ ⎯⎯⎯⎯⎯⎯   ⎯⎯⎯⎯⎯⎯

List of officers' expenses   ⎯⎯⎯⎯⎯⎯

⎯⎯⎯⎯⎯⎯

Other expenses   ⎯⎯⎯⎯⎯⎯

⎯⎯⎯⎯⎯⎯

Miscellaneous   ⎯⎯⎯⎯⎯⎯

   Total anticipated expenditures   ⎯⎯⎯⎯⎯⎯

   Unappropriated balance (emergencies) ⎯⎯⎯⎯⎯⎯

Total   ⎯⎯⎯⎯⎯⎯

When the budget has been completed, it is presented to the organization for adoption or revision. The budget may be considered item by item. A budget requires a majority vote for adoption.

The budget committee cannot recommend expenses in excess of the income and expect to make up the deficit by raising dues. A raise in dues is handled according to the bylaws, and previous notice usually must be given.

Special Committees

A *special committee*, often called an *ad hoc committee*, is a committee appointed or elected to do a specific job. When the committee has completed its task and has given its final report, it is automatically discharged.

A special committee is created by means of a motion. The motion should include the method of selecting the committee, the number of members to be on the committee, and the instructions to the committee. The committee should be appointed to do a specific task.

Subcommittees

Any committee may create a *subcommittee* consisting of its own members to deal with a special aspect of the work of the committee. The subcommittee functions on behalf of the parent committee and is accountable to it.

A subcommittee is an informal group and usually is not given any official recognition by the organization. A subcommittee, unless otherwise provided for, terminates automatically when the term of the parent committee expires.

A *joint committee* is a subcommittee containing representatives of two or more organizations. A joint committee may be established for services that can be more effectively administrated over a wider area than that controlled by a single organization.

Advisory Committee

When there is a need for volunteer assistance in the work of an organization, the board of directors or the executive committee may establish an *advisory committee* or an *advisory council*. The advisory committee generally consists of leaders from professions or representatives of the general public who have made outstanding contributions in their fields. They are appointed as a consultative group. Advisory committees may provide information or otherwise assist the organization in connection with its activities. The committee's actions are not binding on the organization.

Nominating Committee

A *nominating committee* usually is a special committee, although some organizations may establish nominating committees as standing committees. Nominating committees are elected or appointed to nominate persons for offices in an organization. Members on the nominating committee should represent the various interest groups in the organization. The president should have no part in the selection of the committee, nor be an ex-officio member of it.

Nominating committees are responsible for selecting the most capable individuals for each position. They should carefully consider each candidate's dedication to the goals of the organization; how he or she relates to others; and whether he or she is likely to have the time to devote to the office. A candidate must be contacted while the committee is still in session to make sure she or he will serve if nominated and elected. The committee then puts forth the candidate's name at the appropriate general meeting of the organization. (The structure and responsibilities of the nominating committee are covered in greater detail in Chapter 6.)

Auditing Committee

Organizations are concerned about the way their funds are handled. The treasurer's account should be audited at least annually to protect the officers as well as the organization. While some organizations have their books audited by professional auditors, or by certified accountants who may or may not be members of the organization, other organizations appoint an *auditing committee*.

For an audit, the auditing committee needs:

- Copies of the bylaws and standing rules that specify the responsibilities and authority of the treasurer

- The treasurer's books, cancelled checks, receipts, vouchers, current bank statement, and other memos

- Copies of the secretary's minutes documenting authorization for payment of bills

- The budget

Generally, an auditing committee begins by comparing the bank statement at the end of the previous year with the current year's beginning balance. Then total bank deposits are added and total checks paid are deducted. The resulting balance should be the same as the closing bank statement. All cash receipts are then checked to make sure they agree with the bank deposits. Finally, the minutes are examined for approval of payment of bills.

The bank statement, deposits, and paid bills should all agree. If there is a difference, the treasurer should be asked to explain the difference before the auditing committee's report is made.

Credentials Committee

A *credentials committee* is responsible for determining and organizing the representation for a convention. Credentials committees generally are appointed by the president or the executive committee.

Before any convention, the credentials committee provides constituent bodies of the organization with information about how many delegates and alternates the body is entitled to, the eligibility requirements, and the time and manner of their election. Delegates and alternates are required to return credential forms in advance of the convention (see Figure 10.2).

One or two days before the convention opens, the credentials committee supervises *registration*. Registrants present evidence that they are entitled to vote. The credentials committee verifies the members' credentials by checking the credential form files; records their registration; and provides the members with badges, programs, or other necessary materials.

Based on the registration, the credentials committee makes its report as the first item of official business of the convention. The report states the number of delegates with proper credentials registered at a given time.

The committee continues to serve until the end of the convention, in order to record changes in the registration of delegates, to re-register alternates who replace delegates, and to make credentials reports as needed.

Figure 10.2

Sample Credential Form

Name of Organization
Credentials of the Delegate or Alternate

Please print or type   Mail this portion

The members of _____ of _____
                        (name of organization)   (city & state)

Have elected _____ as the delegate and

_____ as the alternate to represent our

_____ at the Annual Convention _____
        (club, unit, region)   (date)

Complete and Return This Half No Later Than (date)

Mail to: _____
                                        signature of delegate

                                   _____
                                        signature of alternate

                                   _____
                                        signature of president

---

Name of Organization
Credential form – Delegate or Alternate

Please print or type

The members of _____ of _____
                        (name of organization)   (city & state)

Have elected _____ as the delegate and

_____ as the alternate to represent our

_____ at the Annual Convention _____
        (club, unit, region)   (date)

Delegate: Please bring   _____
this half to the convention   signature of delegate
and present it properly   _____
signed at the credentials   signature of alternate
desk.   _____
                                        signature of president

Chapter 11

Boards

A *board* is a group of members of an organization, elected or appointed, which is authorized to act for the organization between its meetings. Some common names for boards include: the executive board; the board of directors, governors, trustees, or managers; the cabinet; or the commission. Members of boards are commonly called *directors*.

In some organizations, the directors—other than those elected by the membership—provide for observers to the board who are nonvoting members. In addition, there may be provision for honorary directors, who generally serve in an advisory capacity.

Establishing the Board of Directors

The size of the board of directors varies greatly, depending on the kind of organization and the work involved.

In smaller organizations, the board may consist of less than twelve members. In larger organizations, the board may consist of up to forty members. The criteria for determining the makeup of the board of directors are of great importance. The bylaws of the organization should be specific as to the composition so that it will be balanced. Some organizations stagger membership in the board to prevent a majority of new members at any time.

How Boards Function

A board of directors functions in much the same way as an ordinary committee. The work of the board may be divided among a number of special or permanent committees, each dealing with some phase of the organization's objectives. These committees report back to the board, as they are subordinate to it.

A board cannot appoint an executive committee unless the bylaws so authorize. The executive committee usually is made up of the elected officers. It has the power to act for the board within limitations when the board is not meeting, but it cannot modify any action taken by the board.

Responsibilities of the Board

A board has only the authority given it by the constitution or bylaws, or voted to it by the organization. A board may be granted the power to act for the organization between meetings; however, a board's actions cannot conflict with any action taken by the organization. A board may be authorized to adopt its own rules for the conduct of its business. These rules continue to be in force until they are amended, suspended, or rescinded.

If the bylaws do not state otherwise, a quorum is a majority of the board. If the bylaws provided for a person who is not a member of the organization to be a member of the board, that person has all the rights as other members but is not counted in the quorum.

In nonprofit corporations or organizations, ordinary members may be allowed to vote by proxy. Directors or board members, however, cannot vote by proxy in their meetings. Directors have special responsibilities and powers which they cannot delegate to another individual.

A board of directors is considered to have authority only as a group. Directors as individuals have no legal power except for that delegated to them by the board. However, directors can be held liable as individuals for an action or failure to act as a board member. A board has no power to punish or censure its members. However, it can make a report to the organization.

Board Officers

The officers of the board usually are the officers of the organization, with the president and secretary serving in the same capacity. Some boards include *ex-officio* members. These persons are members of the board by virtue of holding an office or chairing a committee, or because they are members of the parent organization. If an ex-officio member is a member of the organization, he or she has the same rights and obligations as other board members.

If the immediate past president of the organization is an ex-officio member of the board, he or she holds that position until the present president becomes the immediate past president. If the immediate past president dies during his or her tenure as an ex-officio member, that office remains vacant until the current president becomes the immediate past president.

Conducting Board Meetings

Board meetings can vary in length from a few minutes to sessions that seem to end only when each person reaches the point of sheer physical exhaustion. Usually, business in large boards is transacted according to the rules of the assembly. The business should be within the scope and purpose of the organization, unless the bylaws state otherwise.

Agendas

In preparing for a board meeting, the presiding officer's purpose should be to obtain group achievements. An *agenda* should be prepared and given to members in advance of the meeting. This will make clear what subjects will be discussed and how the subjects will affect the members. An agenda should include what the meeting will be about and how long it will last.

Some presiding officers prefer to plan the entire agenda. Others will give the secretary the items of importance and let the secretary add other subjects that should be considered. A typical agenda is illustrated in Figure 11.1.

Figure 11.1

Typical Board Agenda

1. Call to order
2. Reading and approval of minutes
3. Reports of officers
4. Reports of committees
5. Special orders (business postponed to a specific time)
6. Unfinished business and general orders (business postponed to an indefinite time)
7. New business
8. Announcements
9. Closing and adjournment

The presiding officer or secretary may call those who are to attend the meeting and ask if they have anything to place on the agenda. The presiding officer or secretary also should be aware of the concerns of the members of the organization. Such items should be included as items of business. When the advance work is properly done, the board will be able to identify and pinpoint problems and to convert their plans into action.

Other Materials

It often is helpful to circulate copies of the financial statement and previous minutes to board members before each meeting. This gives members the opportunity to review the materials and prepare for discussion. It may be possible to approve the minutes as mailed, thus reducing the length of the board meeting. (See Chapter 4 for further information on minutes.)

Small Boards

Business in a small board should be within the scope and purpose of the organization. The agenda is the same as that of a larger board. Members need not rise to obtain the floor or to make a motion, motions need not be seconded, and there is no limit to the number of times a member can speak to a question. The motion to close debate (previous question) is not allowed.

Generally, informal discussion is permitted without a motion in small boards. If a subject is clear to everyone, it can be agreed to by general consent. Also, the presiding officer can discuss a subject without leaving the chair. However, once a motion is made, it must be voted on under the same rules as in the general assembly.

Meeting by Telephone

In cases when it is impossible to get together to take care of crisis situations, an emergency board meeting may be called by conference call. At least two-thirds of the members must be on the phone, and all formal votes must be taken by roll call. Such a meeting is followed up with the necessary paperwork to support the meeting. The record should reflect:

- Date and time of call

- Purpose of calL

- Names of all members participating

- Roll-call vote

- Signature of person recording the discussion

Emergency action must be ratified at the next business meeting.

Obtaining and approving information from members of the board individually is not the same as approval of the board, since members are not together to hear the same information, discuss, and decide the matter. Even if there is unanimous agreement of the members outside of a properly called meeting, such agreement does not qualify as an act of the board.

Board Reports

The proceedings of the board must be recorded in the *minutes*. These minutes are read and approved by the board. Board minutes generally are not read to the assembly; however, a summary may be given to the assembly.

A board may present a recommendation to the assembly with a motion that it be adopted. It also may present the matter as a resolution. Usually the secretary reads the resolution. No second is required. The presiding officer may ask for discussion on the resolution.

At the annual meeting, the board makes an annual report. All unfinished business of the board dies when a new board assumes its duties.

Chapter 12

The Committee Report

R eports may be called *studies, surveys,* and *opinions.* They may vary in form and substance. Reports may be long or short, formal or informal, special or routine, periodic or serial; they may be typewritten, printed, or given orally.

Since much time is devoted in business meetings to hearing and considering reports, it is important that they be presented in a manner that will bring the most effective results. This chapter outlines some techniques for preparing and presenting effective committee reports.

Preparing Reports

The committee chairperson usually prepares the report and presents it to the committee for acceptance. The committee may make any necessary changes. When the report is deemed satisfactory by the majority of members, the committee adopts it.

When preparing a report, there are three important things to bear in mind: purpose, scope, and audience. These three considerations govern the length, depth, and wording of the report. If the report involves a simple matter, such as the report of a minute-approving committee, the report should be simple and direct. If the report involves a relatively complex matter, such as whether the organization should make major changes in its bylaws, the report should carefully spell out the purpose and consequences of those changes.

Reports also should include the proper *tone*. All committee reports, oral or written, should be in the third person. Formal reports should be impersonal and factual. Informal reports should not be casual; they should be businesslike, stressing the subject. Long reports may be divided into parts or sections with numbered divisions.

Every report should include a clear introduction that includes a statement of the purpose and scope of the report, the method of investigation, or the details of the research. Concise background information, such as a brief history of the problem or previous studies made, also may be given.

Written Reports

Most written reports follow a standard format. They begin with the *heading*, which includes the name of the organization, the title of the report, and the date the report was adopted by the committee.

The *body* of the report follows. It includes an introductory statement, giving the purpose and reason for the report; development of the subject matter through investigation, observation, and materials used; the frequency of committee meetings; and a conclusion, which may contain a recommendation or resolution.

The report concludes with the *signature*. This normally includes simply the signature of the committee chair, with that person's name and title typed below. However, if the report is of considerable importance, all concurring members of the committee include their signatures. (If all concurring members are included, the chair typically signs first and his or her title is omitted.)

Oral Reports

Oral reports should follow the same basic format as written reports. An oral report often may be accompanied by written copies of the report for the official record or even for the members.

It is important to prepare adequately for an oral report. It may be helpful to prepare an outline or speaking notes. The person who will give the report (usually the committee chair) should review the outline or notes several times and perhaps even practice aloud. If the report contains several points or many statistics, it may be helpful to plan visual aids. The speaker should determine what kind of visuals (overhead transparencies, slides, posters, chalkboard notes) will work best in the designated meeting place.

To make an effective oral presentation, speakers should stand and look at the audience. Speakers should state the name of the committee and identify themselves. They should be sure that everyone can hear what is being said. To maintain attention, speakers should try to be positive and enthusiastic. They should have all necessary backup information on hand in order to answer questions from the audience.

Presenting Reports

Normally, either *motions* or *subjects* are referred to committees. When a committee working on a motion is ready to report, the committee chair or someone designated by the chair rises and states, "The committee to which was referred the motion . . . has considered it and has an amendment (*or* substitute motion) to offer." Usually, this report can be made orally, unless the original motion, the amendment, or the substitute motion is quite long or complex.

When a committee working on a subject is ready to report, the report normally should be written. The report should begin: "The committee that was appointed to investigate . . . and to make recommendations, submits the following report." The report ends with: "In conclusion, the committee recommends the adoption of the following: RESOLVED, That . . . ."

The Minority View

Official committee reports present the majority view of the committee. Members of the committee who disagree with the report also may submit their views, although they must do this separately.

After the committee report is presented, the reporting member may say that the minority would like to present its view. The presiding officer may state that the minority view will be heard if there is no objection. If an objection is raised, a member may move that the minority view be heard.

The view of the minority should be in writing. A typical opening for a minority report follows: "The undersigned members, not agreeing with the report of the majority of the committee, submit the following report." The body of the report follows the signatures of the dissenting committee members.

If the committee report contained a resolution or recommendation, the reporting member for the minority view may move to substitute the committee resolution or recommendation with the minority resolution or recommendation.

Disposition of the Report

When the assembly hears a report, that report is *received*. The assembly can take a number of actions on a report that includes a recommendation or a resolution:

1. The report may be referred back to committee if it is not satisfactory, or if it requires further study or modification.

2. The report may be postponed to a more convenient time.

3. The report may be adopted; an adopted report commits the assembly to all findings contained in the report.

4. The report may be adopted in part with exceptions; any resolution or motion in the report may be

amended, although the report itself cannot be amended unless it contains misinformation.

5. The report may be rejected.

Reports containing information are filed, not adopted. A filed report is not binding on the assembly; it is simply available for information.

Appendix

Handbook of Useful Motions

This appendix covers the most commonly used motions, their purpose, and their application. The appendix is arranged in alphabetical order for easy reference.

There are two kinds of motions, *primary* and *secondary*. Primary motions are the main motions (the motions that bring business before the meeting). Secondary motions are procedural and can be considered while a main motion is on the floor. Secondary motions are identified as subsidiary, privileged, and incidental.

Subsidiary motions are always applied to another motion while it is pending and, if adopted, always do something to this other motion. Subsidiary motions have rank. When a motion is before the meeting, any motion is in order if it has a higher precedence or rank than the immediately pending motion; no motion having a lower precedence is in order.

Privileged motions deal with special matters of immediate importance which, without debate, are allowed to interrupt the consideration of anything else. They have no bearing on the subject before the meeting.

Incidental motions apply to the method of transacting business, rather than to the business itself. They relate in different ways to the pending business and deal with questions of procedure arising out of another pending motion. Incidental motions have no rank among themselves. With few exceptions, they are related to the main question in such a way that they must be decided upon immediately, before any business can proceed.

There can be only one main motion on the floor at a time, but it is possible to have several secondary motions on the floor at the same time, provided they are made according to their rank.

Table A.1 lists the order of precedence of motions.

Table A.1

Order of Precedence of Motions—Highest to Lowest

I.   Privileged Motions

   1.   Fix the Time to Which to Adjourn

   2.   Adjourn

   3.   Recess

   4.   Question of Privilege

   5.   Call for the Orders of the Day

II.   Subsidiary Motions

   6.   Lay on the Table

   7.   Previous Question

   8.   Limit or Extend Debate

   9.   Postpone Definitely

  10.   Commit or Refer

  11.   Amend

  12.   Postpone Indefinitely

III.   Main Motions (no order of precedence)

   Discharge a Committee

   Ratify

   Reconsider

   Rescind

   Take from the Table

IV.   Incidental Motions (no order of precedence)

Appeal

Consider by Paragraph or Seriatim

Division of a Question

Division of the Assembly

Motions Relating to Nominations

Motions Relating to the Polls and Methods of
    Voting

Motions That Are Requests

Object to the Consideration of a Question

Point of Order

Suspend the Rules

Withdraw

Adjourn

A privileged motion. This motion is made to terminate a
meeting.

Forms of the Motion

"I move that we adjourn."

"I move to adjourn."

"I move that we adjourn at 8 o'clock."

"I move that when we adjourn, we adjourn to meet at
the same time tomorrow evening."

Rules Governing the Motion

1. Cannot interrupt a speaker
2. Requires recognition
3. Is not debatable
4. Is not amendable
5. Requires a majority vote
6. May not be reconsidered

After the motion to adjourn has been moved, the following parliamentary steps are in order while the motion to adjourn is pending, or after the meeting has voted to adjourn:

1. Inform the members of business requiring attention before adjournment
2. Make important announcements
3. Make (but not take up) a motion to reconsider a previous vote
4. Give notice of a motion to be made at the next meeting (or on the next day of a convention) where the motion requires previous notice
5. Move to set the time for an adjourned meeting if the time for the next meeting is not already settled

The meeting is not closed until the chair has declared that the meeting is adjourned. Members should not leave their seats until the chair says, "The meeting is adjourned."

A meeting can be adjourned without a motion if the time for adjournment has arrived. The chair simply announces that the meeting is adjourned. When it appears that there is no further business, the chair may say, "There being no further business, the meeting is adjourned."

Adopt

An incidental motion. The expressions *adopt, accept,* and *agree to* are all equivalent. It is best to use the word *adopt.*

Forms of the Motion

"I move that we adopt the recommendation of the committee."

"I move that the auditor's report be adopted."

Rules Governing the Motion

1. Cannot interrupt a speaker
2. Requires recognition
3. Requires a second
4. Is debatable
5. Is amendable
6. Requires a majority vote
7. May be reconsidered

Amend

A subsidiary motion. This motion is made to change the wording of the motion before final action is taken on it.

There are two kinds of amendments, the primary (first degree) and the secondary (second degree) amendments. The primary amendment amends the pending motion and must be germane to it, that is, closely related to the motion. The secondary amendment amends the primary amendment and must be germane to it. Secondary amendments do not apply to the main motion. Only two amendments may be pending at one time. After they have been disposed of, another amendment may be made, if it is germane. When there are two amendments pending, the secondary amendment is voted on first, then the primary amendment. The main motion is then open for discussion before the final vote is taken.

Forms of the Motion

"I move to amend the motion by adding at the end . . . ."

"I move to amend the motion by striking out the word (or words) between . . . and . . . ."

"I move to insert the word (or words) between the word . . . and the word . . . ."

"I move to amend the motion by striking out the word (or words) and inserting the word (or words) between the word . . . and the word . . . ."

"I move to strike out the main motion and insert . . . ."

"I move to substitute the following . . . ."

Rules Governing the Motion

1. Is not in order when another has the floor

2. Requires recognition

3. Requires a second

4. Is debatable when applied to a debatable motion

5. Is amendable (a primary amendment is amendable; a secondary amendment is not)

6. Yields to higher ranking subsidiary motins and all privileged and applicable incidental motions, except motions to divide and to consider by paragraph or seriatim.

7. Requires a majority vote even if the motion to be amended requires a higher vote (a primary amendment requires two votes, the first on the amendment and the second on the pending main motion; a secondary amendment requires three votes, the first on the secondary amendment, the second on the primary amendment, and the third on the pending main motion)

8. May be reconsidered

Amend Something Previously Adopted

A specific main motion. This is a motion by which an action previously adopted or taken can be changed, repealed, or annulled.

Forms of the Motion

"I move to amend the motion adopted at the January meeting by striking out . . . . Previous notice was given at the last meeting."

"I move to amend the motion relating to . . . adopted at the May meeting by inserting . . . . Previous notice has been given."

Rules Governing the Motion

1. Cannot interrupt a speaker

2. Requires recognition

3. Requires a second

4. Is debatable; debate may go into the merits of the motion which it is proposed to amend

5. Is amendable

6. Requires a two-thirds vote or a vote of a majority of the entire membership, except when notice has been given at a previous meeting; then the motion requires a majority vote

7. Only the negative vote may be reconsidered

Appeal

An incidental motion. This motion allows a member who disagrees with the ruling of the chair to have the assembly make the decision.

Form of the Motion

"I appeal from the decision of the chair."

Rules Governing the Motion

1. Is in order when another member has the floor; must be proposed immediately
2. Does not require recognition
3. Requires a second
4. Is debatable
5. Is not amendable
6. Requires a majority vote in the negative to overrule the chair's decision (a majority vote or tie vote sustains the decision of the chair)
7. Takes precedence over any question and must be decided immediately

Call for the Orders of the Day

A privileged motion. This motion requires that the assembly conform to its agenda, program, or order of business, or that it take up a general or special order due to come up.

When the orders of the day are called for, the chair may say, "Would the assembly care to finish this part of the business before adhering to the orders of the day?" If there is an affirmative vote, the business is completed before returning to the agenda.

Form of the Motion

"I call for the orders of the day."

Rules Governing the Motion

1. Is in order when another has the floor

2. Does not require recognition

3. Does not require a second

4. Is not debatable

5. Is not amendable

6. Upon the call by a single member, the chair must take up the prescribed order of business; no vote is necessary

7. Cannot be reconsidered

Close Debate

A subsidiary motion. This motion is to prevent or to stop discussion on the pending question or questions and to bring the pending question to an immediate vote.

Forms of the Motion

"I move to close debate on the motion."

"I move to close debate on all pending motions."

Rules Governing the Motion

1. Cannot interrupt a speaker

2. Requires recognition

3. Requires a second

4. Is not debatable

5. Is not amendable

6. Requires a two-thirds vote

7. Can be applied to debatable motions only

Close Nominations

An incidental motion. A nomination is a formal presentation of the member's name as a candidate for a particular office. When there are several candidates for an office, a member may wish to close nominations.

In cases when it appears that there are no further nominations for a particular office, the chair declares the nomination closed, or someone may move to close nominations. Usually no motion is necessary to close nominations, since they may be reopened by a motion to this effect.

Form of the Motion

"I move to close nominations."

Rules Governing the Motion

1. Cannot interrupt a speaker

2. Requires recognition

3. Requires a second

4. Is not debatable

5. Is amendable

6. Requires a two-thirds vote.

Commit *or* Refer

A subsidiary motion. This motion is made to refer a pending motion to one or more persons. This motion may be applied to a main motion or to a main motion with adhering amendments.

Forms of the Motion

"I move to refer the question to a committee."

"I move to refer the motion to the . . . committee."

"I move to refer the motion to a committee of three appointed by the chair."

"I move to refer the question to the executive committee with power to act."

Rules Governing the Motion

1. Cannot interrupt a speaker

2. Requires recognition

3. Requires a second

4. Is debatable as to the desirability of committing and to the appropriate details of the motion to commit

5. Is amendable as to the committee composition, manner of composition, and instructions to the committee

6. Requires a majority vote

7. Can be reconsidered if the committee has not begun consideration of the question

Consider Informally

A subsidiary motion. This motion allows the members to speak informally on a motion. If this motion passes, the question is open to informal consideration. There is no limit to the number of times a member can speak on the question or on any amendment. As soon as the question has been voted upon, the informal consideration ceases.

Form of the Motion

"I move that we discuss this subject informally."

Rules Governing the Motion

1. Cannot interrupt a speaker

2. Requires recognition

3. Requires a second

4. Is debatable

5. Is not amendable

6. Requires a majority vote

Consider by Paragraph

An incidental motion. This motion provides for long motions or reports consisting of several paragraphs, resolutions, or sections to be considered by opening different parts to debate and amendment separately, without dividing the question.

Each paragraph is open to debate and amendment if the motion to consider by paragraph is adopted. When no further amendments are proposed and debate ceases on that paragraph, the chair proceeds to the next paragraph until all have been open to debate and amendment. After all paragraphs are amended, the entire series is open to further amendment and debate. At this time additional parts may be inserted or parts may be struck out. A single vote is then taken on the adoption of the entire series.

Forms of the Motion

"I move that the resolution be considered by paragraph."

"I move that the bylaws be considered by sections."

Rules Governing the Motion

1. Cannot interrupt a speaker
2. Requires recognition
3. Requires a second
4. Is not debatable
5. Is amendable
6. Requires a majority vote
7. Cannot be reconsidered

Discharge a Committee

A specific main motion. This is a motion by means of which further consideration of a subject may be taken away from a committee. The assembly can take the matter out of a committee's hands after it has been referred to it and before the committee has made a final report. So long as a question (subject) is in the hands of a committee, the assembly cannot consider another motion involving practically the same thing.

No motion is necessary to discharge a committee when the committee has given its final report to the assembly. The committee is then automatically discharged from further consideration of the matter.

Forms of the Motion

"I move that the committee to which was referred the motion regarding ... be discharged."

"I move that the committee appointed to investigate the question of . . . be discharged and that this matter be made a special order of business at our next meeting."

"I move that the membership committee be discharged from further consideration of the motion referred to it on . . . ."

Rules Governing the Motion

1. Cannot interrupt a speaker

2. Requires recognition

3. Requires a second

4. Is debatable; debate may go into the merits of the question which is in the hands of the committee

5. Is amendable by the basic process of amending, and may instruct the committee instead of discharging it

6. Requires a two-thirds vote, or a vote of the majority of the entire membership, or only a majority vote if previous notice has been given at a previous meeting or in the call to the meeting

7. Only the negative vote may be reconsidered

Division of the Assembly

An incidental motion. This motion is used when a member doubts the result of a vote announced by the chair. A division must be called for before the chair states another motion. If a member wants the vote to be counted, he or she must make a motion to that effect.

Forms of the Motion

"I call for a division."

"Division."

Rules Governing the Motion

1. Can interrupt a speaker

2. Does not require recognition

3. Is not debatable

4. Is not amendable

5. Does not require a vote, since a single member can demand that a vote be taken by standing

Division of the Question

An incidental motion. The purpose of this motion is to divide a motion or an amendment if it consists of two or more parts, each part being capable of standing alone.

The motion must state clearly the manner in which the question is to be divided. A motion cannot be divided unless each part presents a proper question for the assembly to act on if none of the other parts is adopted. A resolution cannot be divided if it contains several parts which would be impossible to separate without rewriting the resolution.

Forms of the Motion

"I move to divide the motion so as to consider separately the . . . and the . . . ."

"I move to divide the resolution so as to consider separately the question on . . . and the question on . . . ."

Rules Governing the Motion

1. Cannot interrupt a speaker

2. Requires recognition

3. Requires a second

4. Is not debatable

5. Is amendable

6. Requires a majority vote

7. Cannot be reconsidered

Lay on the Table (Temporarily)

A subsidiary motion. This motion puts aside the pending question temporarily when something more urgent arises. The motion to lay on the table cannot be qualified in any way. The motion to use is to postpone to a certain time.

When the motion is laid on the table, all adhering motions go with it. When taken from the table, the motion comes back exactly as it was, with all the adhering motions.

The motion to lay on the table may be taken from the table on the same day, provided that some other business has taken place. If the motion is not taken from the table at the close of the next regular business meeting, the question dies. However, the matter can be taken up as new business at a later meeting.

Forms of the Motion

"I move to lay the question on the table."

"I move that the resolution be laid on the table."

Rules Governing the Motion

1. Cannot interrupt a speaker

2. Requires recognition

3. Requires a second

4. Is not debatable; however, a member may make a short statement as to the reason for making the motion

5. Is not amendable

6. Requires a majority vote

Limit or Extend Debate

A subsidiary motion. This motion is to limit the time that will be devoted to the discussion of a pending question, or to lengthen the time of discussion.

Forms of the Motion

"I move to limit debate on the motion to one hour."

"I move to limit the time of each speaker on the motion to three minutes."

"I move that the time of the speaker be extended by ten minutes."

Rules Governing the Motion

1. Cannot interrupt a speaker

2. Requires recognition

3. Is not debatable

4. Is amendable only as to time

5. Requires a two-thirds vote

6. Can be reconsidered

Main Motion

The main motion brings a subject before the assembly for its discussion and decision.

Motions that can be made while the main motion is pending include: all subsidiary and all privileged motions; and applicable incidental motions, such as: division of the question, consider by paragraph, withdraw, object to the consideration of an original main motion.

A main motion should be stated in the affirmative, since the negative form often confuses members in voting. Avoid saying, "I move that we do not increase our dues." The motion can be clearly stated by saying, "I move that our dues remain the same." A main motion should be concise, clear, and made as complete as possible so as to avoid amendments.

Forms of the Motion

"I move that we establish a scholarship fund."

"I move the adoption of the following resolution, RESOLVED: That . . . ."

Rules Governing the Motion

1. Cannot interrupt a speaker

2. Requires recognition

3. Requires a second

4. Is debatable

5. Is amendable

6. Yields to all subsidiary, privileged, or applicable incidental motions

7. Requires a majority vote, except when the bylaws require a greater vote; when adoption would have the effect of suspending a rule of order or a parliamentary right; or when adoption would have the effect of rescinding or amending something previously adopted

8. May be reconsidered

Method of Voting

An incidental motion. This motion is used when some form other than voice vote is desired.

Form of the Motion

"I move that when we vote, we vote by ballot."

Rules Governing the Motion

1. Cannot interrupt a speaker

2. Requires recognition

3. Requires a second

4. Is not debatable

5. Is amendable

6. Requires a majority vote

Object to the Consideration of a Question

An incidental motion. This motion is used to avoid a particular embarrassing or undesirable original main motion from being discussed. If an objection is sustained, the motion is not before the assembly.

Form of the Motion

"I object to the consideration of the motion (resolution)."

Rules Governing the Motion

1. Can interrupt proceedings; must be made before the chair states the motion and before any debate

2. Does not require a second

3. Is not debatable

4. Is not amendable

5. Requires two-thirds vote against consideration to sustain the objection

Parliamentary Inquiry

An incidental motion. The purpose of this motion is to enable a member to ask the chair a question of procedure in connection with the pending question or with a motion that the member wishes to bring before the assembly immediately. It is also used to ask for information on the effect of the pending question.

Form of the Motion

"I rise to a parliamentary inquiry."

Rules Governing the Motion

1. Can interrupt a speaker if it requires an immediate answer

2. Requires no second

3. Is not debatable

4. Is not amendable

5. Requires no vote

6. Can have no motion applied to it

Point of Order

An incidental motion. This motion is to call to the attention of the chair a violation of a rule when the chair neglects to call it.

A point of order must be raised immediately. It cannot be brought up later unless the error involved a violation of the bylaws. The motion interrupts business. The presiding officer either rules that the point of order is well taken and orders the mistake or omission to be corrected, or rules that the point of order is not well taken and resumes business at the point where it was interrupted.

Forms of the Motion

"I rise to a point of order."

"Point of order."

Rules Governing the Motion

1. Can interrupt a speaker

2. Does not require recognition

3. Does not require a second

4. Is not debatable

5. Is not amendable

6. Does not require a vote as the chair decides; if submitted to the assembly, a majority vote is required

7. May not be reconsidered

Postpone Definitely (to a Certain Time)

A subsidiary motion. This is a motion by which action on a pending question can be put off, within limits, to a definite day, meeting, or hour, or until a certain event.

There are limits on postponement. A question can be postponed only until the close of the next session. In a convention, a motion may not be postponed beyond the last meeting of the convention.

Forms of the Motion

"I move to postpone consideration of the motion until 3 P.M."

"I move to postpone the question until our next meeting."

"I move to postpone consideration of this question until our next meeting, and that it be made a special order for 1:30 P.M."

Rules Governing the Motion

1. Cannot interrupt a speaker

2. Requires recognition

3. Requires a second

4. Is debatable only as to the propriety and details of postponement

5. Is amendable only as to time to which the question is to be postponed

6. Requires a majority vote in its simple form; requires a two-thirds vote if made a special order

7. Can be reconsidered

Previous Question (Stop Debate)

A subsidiary motion. The motion "previous question" is often misunderstood. It is a motion to stop debate and take an immediate vote on the pending question. Members sometimes call out "Question" without obtaining the floor. This is discourteous and disorderly.

If the previous question is adopted, votes are taken immediately on the question specified. If lost, debate continues on the immediately pending question.

Forms of the Motion

"I move to vote immediately on the motion."

"I move to vote now on all pending questions."

"I move the previous question."

Rules Governing the Motion

1. Cannot interrupt a speaker

2. Requires recognition

3. Requires a second

4. Is not debatable

5. Is not amendable

6. Requires a two-thirds vote

Question of Privilege

A privileged motion. This motion enables a member to secure immediate decision and action by the presiding officer on a request that concerns the comfort, convenience, rights, or privileges of the assembly or of the member. It is also used to request permission to present a motion of urgent nature, even though business is pending.

Forms of the Motion

"I rise to a question of privilege of the assembly."

"I rise to a question of personal privilege."

Rules Governing the Motion

1. Can interrupt a speaker if it requires an immediate answer

2. Does not require recognition

3. Is not debatable

4. Is not amendable

5. Requires no vote

6. Chair rules; ruling is subject to appeal

7. May not be reconsidered

8. Can have no motion applied to it except the motion to withdraw

Ratify

A specific main motion. To ratify means to approve, confirm, validate, or make legal. The object of the motion is to approve or legalize an action taken in an emergency or when no quorum was present.

Forms of the Motion

"I move to ratify the action taken by the executive committee."

"I move that we ratify the action taken by . . . ."

Action already taken cannot become legally valid until approved by the assembly. The assembly can ratify such actions of its officers, committees, and delegates as it would have the right to authorize in advance. It cannot make valid a voice vote election when the bylaws require elections by ballot, nor can it ratify anything done in violation of national, state, or local law.

Rules Governing the Motion

1. Cannot interrupt a speaker

2. Requires recognition

3. Requires a second

4. Is debatable

5. Is amendable

6. Requires a majority vote

7. Can be reconsidered

Recess

A privileged motion. Recess is a short intermission in the assembly's proceedings which does not close the meeting, and after which business will be resumed at exactly where it was interrupted.

When a motion to recess is made when no business is pending, it is a main motion. When a recess is provided for in the adopted program, the chair, without further action by the assembly, announces the fact and declares the assembly to be in recess when that time comes. If the chair fails to announce the recess at that time, a member may call for the orders of the day.

Forms of the Motion

"I move that we recess for ten minutes."

"I move to recess untill 2:30 P.M."

Rules Governing the Motion

1. Cannot interrupt a speaker

2. Requires recognition

3. Requires a second

4. Is not debatable

5. Is amendable as to the length of time of the recess

6. Requires a majority vote

7. May be reconsidered

Reconsider

A specific main motion. The purpose of the motion to reconsider a vote taken on a motion is to bring that motion again before the assembly, as though no vote had been taken on it.

The motion to reconsider can be made only on the same day or the next calendar day after the original vote was taken.

Form of the Motion

"I move to reconsider the vote taken on the motion relating to . . . ."

Rules Governing the Motion

1. Cannot interrupt a speaker
2. Requires recognition
3. Requires a second
4. Is debatable
5. Is not amendable
6. Requires a majority vote
7. Cannot be reconsidered

Rescind

A specific main motion. The purpose of the motion is to repeal (cancel, void) a main motion passed at a previous meeting. The effect of the motion to rescind is to strike out an entire motion, resolution, rule, or paragraph that has been adopted at some previous meeting. However, there is some action which cannot be rescinded. When something has been done as a result of a vote on the motion, it is impossible to undo it.

Form of the Motion

"I move to rescind the motion passed at the May meeting concerning . . . ."

Rules Governing the Motion

1. Cannot interrupt a speaker

2. Requires recognition

3. Requires a second

4. Is debatable and opens the motion it proposes to rescind to debate

5. Cannot be amended

6. Requires a majority vote with previous notice

Suspend the Rules

An incidental motion. This motion is used when the assembly wishes to do something that cannot be done without violating its own rules, but which does not conflict with the constitution or bylaws, local, state, or national laws, or with the fundamental rules of parliamentary procedure.

Rules that may not be suspended include: rules contained in the bylaws, constitution, or charter, unless that particular document specifies for its own suspension; rules protecting absentees or basic rights of the individual members.

Rules that may be suspended include: rules of order (parliamentary procedure) by a two-thirds vote; standing rules (rules that do not relate to parliamentary procedure, such as hours for meetings to begin or end).

Forms of the Motion

"I move to suspend rule number five."

"I move to suspend the rule which interferes with . . . ."

"I move to suspend the rule in order to take up . . . ."

Rules Governing the Motion

1. Cannot interrupt a speaker

2. Requires recognition

3. Requires a second

4. Is not debatable

5. Is not amendable

6. Requires a two-thirds vote

7. Can have no motions applied to it except to withdraw

8. Must be decided immediately

Take from the Table

A specific main motion. This motion is used when it is desired to bring back for further consideration a motion that was laid on the table.

Forms of the Motion

"I move to take from the table the motion relating to . . . ."

Rules Governing the Motion

1. Cannot interrupt a speaker
2. Requires recognition
3. Requires a second
4. Is not debatable
5. Is not amendable
6. Requires a majority vote
7. Cannot be reconsidered

Withdraw a Motion

An incidental motion. This motion allows a member who proposed a motion to remove it from consideration by the assembly. The consent of the seconder is not necessary. A motion can be withdrawn if there is no objection, or with permission from the assembly, up to the moment the final vote is taken.

Forms of the Motion

"I withdraw my motion." (before the motion has been stated by the chair)

"I request permission to withdraw my motion." (after the motion has been stated and discussed)

Rules Governing the Motion

1. Cannot interrupt a speaker

2. Requires recognition

3. Requires no second, as it is a request

4. Is not debatable

5. Is not amendable

6. Requires no vote

7. Can apply to all motions

Index